CHOIR OF MUSES

CHOIR OF MUSES

Etienne Gilson

CLUNY

Providence, Rhode Island

Cluny Media edition, 2018

This Cluny edition may include minor editorial revisions to the original text.
For more information regarding this title
or any other Cluny Media publication,
please write to info@clunymedia.com, or to
Cluny Media, P.O. Box 1664, Providence, RI, 02901

VISIT US ONLINE AT WWW.CLUNYMEDIA.COM

Translations by Maisie Ward

TRANSLATOR'S NOTE:
For the epigraph, I have ventured to print this poem
because it fits so surprisingly the theme of M. Gilson's book.

ISBN: 978-1944418755

Cover design by Clarke & Clarke
Cover image: Gustav Klimpt, *Music*,
1895, oil on canvas (detail)
Courtesy of Wikimedia Commons

Contents

Possession

A Poet loved a Star,
And to it whispered nightly,
"Being so fair, why art thou, love, so far?
Or why so coldly shine, who shin'st so brightly?
O Beauty wooed and unpossest!
Oh, might I to this beating breast
But clasp thee once, and then die blest!"
That Star her Poet's love,
So wildly warm, made human;
And leaving, for his sake, her heaven above
His Star stooped earthward, and became a Woman.
"Thou who hast wooed and hast possest,
My lover answer: Which was best,
The Star's beam or the Woman's breast?"
"I miss from heaven," the man replied,
"A light that drew my spirit to it."
And to the man the woman sighed,
"I miss from earth a poet."

– *Robert Bulwer Lytton (Owen Meredith)*

1. The Problem of the Muses

"We must admit, said he, that the Muses gave a good answer. Of course, I retorted, because they are Muses."

– Plato, *Republic* (VIII, 547a)

A historian attacks the subject of the Muses nervously and with some fear of being laughed at. Weighted with quotations and authorities, dull and stumbling, what favors can such as he hope for from these goddesses? Still, one of them is Clio, the Muse of History. The endless gossip of that old lady is a timely reminder that she is never content merely "to make researches," to "undertake an investigation." If she stopped at that, she would not write so many huge books. Clio is a Muse simply because she invents endlessly and, as indeed she boasts in her franker moments, re-creates the past.

ETIENNE GILSON

We have only one word—history—for what are in fact two things: the history that happened and the history that is told. It is as though the word "physics" meant, at the same time, nature itself and the knowledge that we have of nature. Indeed that would be less bad, for even those who know nothing of physics have nature in front of them: they are in no risk of confusing the two. But the history that happened only exists, for us, hidden inside the history that describes it. While it is happening it is not being told. When Clio begins to talk, if only a moment later, what she is talking about has ceased to be.

For this reason Clio invents, restores, manufactures. In any event it all passes through her imagination, which is why she is a Muse. This is so true that when science itself attempts the impossible and offers an objective knowledge of what no longer exists, it becomes transformed into "the history of nature" and borrows its inspiration from Clio. Then we get magnificent poems such as the *Timaeus* of Plato, *Le Monde* of Descartes (which has been called nature's novel), to say nothing of those strange cosmologies of today which juggle with thousands of millions of years and tell us about the first beginnings of life or the evolution of species exactly as though the men who are talking had seen it all themselves. These are our modern epics, and they are very enjoyable to read. But we cannot take them wholly seriously when we remember the accounts other people give of things that have happened to ourselves. Their stories are always probable—and false in proportion to their likelihood. Everything ought to have happened to us as they tell it, it would have been far more rational. But it was not like that at all: things happened in a different way and for different reasons—often because of a series of those improbable mix-ups of which life is full. These things could be guessed by no outside observer, and would make history impossible if history included them in its scope, for they disappear without leaving a trace behind them.

2

But if Clio is in difficulties over events, she is utterly help-less when it comes to thought and feelings. General probabilities, a sort of similarity based upon the constant element in human nature, certainly permit guesses that may approximate to what a man thought or felt in a given situation. We may get pretty close, we may in a general way guess the motives on which he acted, but the chances of error are enormous. Individual psychology is a barrier that history cannot cross. No one knows this better than a man who tries to talk about himself, to put a little shape into his own story, so as not to be lost in the labyrinth of his own mind—a labyrinth in which future historians will claim to be more at home than he ever was himself.

Thus it is that, in speaking about certain poets and their Muses, one can lay no claim to objectivity. The chances are minute of getting the story exactly right. All that I can hope for, besides the pleasure of talking about what interests me, is to focus attention on certain human situations and experiences, complex enough to tempt me to reduce them to one or another of their elements, but with qualities sufficiently definite of their own to make it possible to study them individually. To explain them would be quite another matter, but it will be something anyhow to have shown that, with all our talk of them, we can still only guess what it all meant to the men and women concerned.

The Muses are primarily divinities invented by the Greeks to account for that ordered design which confers upon certain of the ideas and works of men a superhuman loveliness. There was a Muse for dancing, a Muse for tragedy, even one for astron-omy. I will not mention their names for fear of spoiling the parlor game which you win if you remember the whole list. But notice this: the Ancients, by appointing goddesses for the great forms of art and the principal kinds of learning, were expressing under material images that religious feeling which, even among those who call themselves—nay, who really are—atheists, will always be involved in the creation of great works of art. When he ceases to be a mere manufacturer, the artist speaks in the language of religion.

But these are not the Muses I am going to discuss. Besides signifying the divine source of inspiration, the word is often used for inspiration itself, or to quote Plato, the frenzy, the state of possession, that arises from it. "When inspiration seizes upon a pure and sensitive spirit," says Plato in the *Phaedrus*, "it awakens and inspires it; and by exalting in odes and poems of all kinds the numberless great achievements of the Ancients, becomes the education of their descendants. But one on whom the Muses have not breathed frenzy, who comes to the portals of Poetry convinced that art is all he needs to make him a good poet, will not achieve perfection. The poetry of good sense is eclipsed by the poetry of inspiration." Eternal, immutable truth. Boileau had but to turn it into verse—"In vain to Parnassus a foolhardy author...." Even Valéry himself never denies this, for it is equally true that without "enthusiasm" a poet has nothing to say, and that "enthusiasm" is not part of a writer's equipment—it must come to him. Hence we mortals, too humble for the company of the nine daughters of Jupiter and Mnemosyne, use the term "Muse" for the inspiration they bestow upon poets, artists, or creators of great works of the mind.

In this sense a poet's muse may mean his inspiration in general or the special character of his poetic genius: thus we might speak of the muse of Racine or the muse of Victor Hugo. These men may be called the lovers, the darlings, or the nurslings of the muses; but of any real poet we say that he is visited by his muse. When an artist is a woman she herself is even spoken of as a Muse—for the men of today, having lost the meaning of religion, tend to turn woman into a divinity: and there is no great point in criticizing a custom which the women of today are working so hard to be rid of. These women Muses are still on the increase, but it is not of them that this book treats. My concern is not with women themselves inspired, or with the inspiration that moves them, but with the women who have inspired men to write.

Like the Muses who write, these also are women; but like goddesses they breathe forth inspiration, so that they almost have a right to the capital letter that adorns the title of a divinity. In principle these Muses are beautiful, and doubtless they were often so in reality—no trouble at all to believe it of those in the far past of whom we have no portraits. It is enough that they were beautiful in the eyes of their poets: and this may comfort us for not being able to study their portraiture as it objectively was— for indeed those who loved these ladies never did look at them objectively. Of the earliest—Beatrice and Laura—no portraits have survived. Of those nearer our time we do possess pictures, but what is a portrait compared with a living reality? The most magnificent canvas, the most living statute, does not reveal the constant play of feature, the walk, the notes of the voice, or above all, as with Beatrice, the smile that belongs to Muses alone and lives perpetually in their gaze. You feel that the poets who loved them saw them once and for all, or at least that that first sight was made eternal for them, living on through every later appearance. It was the one true vision, the one they always somehow saw. It has often enough been said that love lives on a first vision— of which the lover seeks through every possible device to make the thrill eternal. Rousseau even maintained the paradox that you can only remain faithful by deceiving the woman you love, because she is forever changing, and to love her as she is, is to be unfaithful to her as she was. The full meaning of his thesis is apparent to the man who as an artist identifies the beloved with that first overwhelming vision of his Inspiration. Villiers de l'Isle-Adam has admirably described in *Eve Future* man's need to rediscover that first unique hour, all other hours being sweet only in the measure that they prolong or recall it: "Can one ever be tired of re-living that unique delight: that wonderful changeless hour! The loved one's whole meaning in that hour—we are forever striving to experience it anew, to call it back to life. All other hours are coins minted from that hour of gold." But how mint them if the reality of every day gives the lie to that hour, a lie that grows crueller as the years go by? Villiers is utterly right: if a pact were possible, for the beloved to remain as she was at this unique meeting, and for the poet himself never to change, it would be no play-acting to make it. But it is impossible to bring those moments back if you have lived through others that give the lie to them. The beloved must have no personality of her own, or the dream will not last. Villiers certainly never went deeper in his analysis of his "ideal Beatrix" than when he made Edison remark to Lord Ewald that at heart he did not want to see her face—and how right he was. To be constantly forced to look at the real face as it alters is no help toward finding the woman who lives on in the poet's dream.

And if it is so hard for the poet to bring his vision back to life, how can we imagine her for ourselves? The *Femme mordue par un serpent* comes too early, and Ricard's portrait comes too late, to restore for us the features of the woman who was Baudelaire's Muse. Even should I see her as she was when he first looked upon her, I should not see her through his eyes. It was to Petrarch alone that a dazzling golden-haired girl appeared that morning in the church at Avignon. Everyone could see *her*, but only he could see the Muse of a *Canzoniere*. The portraits we possess of Muses deceive us, not because they show them as more or less beautiful than they were, but because they were wholly other. In this field even our disillusionments remain illusions.

This is no reason for not looking at the Muses, especially as the species, if unlikely to disappear, may very well undergo change. The future is perhaps designing for our grandchildren small, muscular, sporting Muses, skillfully piloting their airplanes—or perhaps long-limbed girls of the sort that unauthorized juries raise to the fleeting dignity of Miss Lithuania or Miss America. The Muses of past years had a likeness to one another and seem to have been chosen from quite a different species. This may be a mere question of period and style, but even if it is accidental and temporary it remains a fact; and it applies, curiously enough, to the supposed portraits as well as to the real ones. Look at Laura, at Madame Sabatier, at Marie d'Agoult, at Mathilde Wesendonk: in whatever fashion they are dressed, they may be dreamers but they are not dream-women—nice creatures, rather, who gaze at us a little sadly but always tranquilly, as though in search of an orphan to adopt rather than of a lover to seduce. It would be unwise to trust them too far, since still waters run deep and sensuality might awaken in the end and spoil it all; but none can doubt of the order and beauty of their living, or even of a certain affluence—without which worldly tranquillity remains precarious. Those Muses meant for their poets not so much the promise of amorous adventure as the nostalgic luxury of sanctuary. Nothing that exists is quite pure, not even the soul of an artist. He regrets and covets that bourgeois life of ease and comfort which he renounced to follow the call of his art. Sometimes he is so jealous of it that he destroys it when he meets it—thus getting no real benefit from it: for it is hopeless to think he can have art and the sacrifices it demands, a transcendent spiritual communion between the artist and his Muse, and, in the same life and with the same woman, a lover pouring out her love for the rebuilding of the threatened edifice of home and family.

We must never forget the background of these stories: if so many Muses were married women, mothers of children, and a good deal richer than their poets, it is because the most footloose vagrants of artistic adventure keep in their hearts the longing for a home.

When all is said and done, however mingled the feelings they inspire in us, we cannot examine these stories without coming to see that every Muse is for the poet what Boethius once described as an image of the real good, an image which cannot bring us to beatitude, or, in Dante's splendid translation, one of those "false images which never fully keep their promise." This experience is so often repeated that the promise which cannot be kept rings in our ears today as the reminder of a whole tradition.

Yet without this promise there would hardly be great art. More humanly complex than the poet admits or suspects, his meeting with the Muse appears to him a simple experience: in the beauty of a woman he has had the revelation of absolute beauty, and in its service must sacrifice all. It is the overwhelming, transforming experience of which Plato in *Phaedrus* has given a description that applies to men of all periods. Were there in it only the desire for physical possession, this would be nothing uncommon, nothing to rivet our attention. But if there were no desire—or at least the emotional stirring which precedes desire—the thing would be not so much experience as contemplation. In the figurative language of a myth Plato describes something quite special, something which happens only to those whose mind has long been focused upon the spiritual but who suddenly, to their own great amazement, experience in a powerful bodily emotion the immediate presence of the divine:

"But he whose initiation is recent, and who has been the spectator of many glories in the other world, is amazed when he sees anyone having a godlike face or form, which is the expression of divine beauty;" and at first a shudder runs through him, and again the old awe steals over him; then looking upon the face of his beloved as of a god he reverences him, and if he were not afraid of being thought a downright madman, he would sacrifice to his beloved as to the image of a god; then while he gazes on him there is a sort of reaction, and the shudder passes into an unusual heat and perspiration; for, as he receives the effluence of beauty through the eyes, the wing moistens and he warms. And as he warms, the parts out of which the wing grew, and which had been hitherto closed and rigid, and had prevented the wing from shooting forth, are melted, and as nourishment streams upon him, the lower end of the wings begins to swell and grow from the root upwards; and the growth extends under the whole soul—for once the whole was winged."[1]

How many poets will instantly recognize in different forms the substance of this description. Here is the "thunderbolt" that hurls the poet to the ground before the woman who is to become his Muse. True, Plato was thinking of boys, but since Christianity restored nature to its rights men have ceased to blush at being moved by women's beauty. And from the angle of our discussion the thing that sets Eros on fire matters little, since it is only the occasion of his burning, not the object for which he burns. The love Plato is discussing in *Phaedrus* means for him above all else an imperious summons to rise through things sensible to the intelligible. The occasion of this love, therefore, matters little—whatever it may be, the love must pass beyond what stirred it. Those of our contemporaries who justify homosexuality by proclaiming it the traditional source of great art are entirely

---

1.   *Greek Literature in Translation*, eds. Whitney J. Oates and Charles T. Murphy (Philadelphia: David Mckay Company, 1967), pp. 503–4 (Plato, *Phaedrus*).

mistaken in their references to Plato. Pederasty practiced inspires no masterpieces. There is no relation between what the inspired lover of Phaedrus is seeking, and whatever these men get out of their bleak fornicating. Reduced to terms of the human experience it is interpreting, the Platonic doctrine of Eros expresses not a thesis but a fact. The love called Platonic has no need of Plato to be constantly discovered by men for themselves. It lives on by its own power. Moreover, even according to Plato it needs continence to achieve its highest form, for it does not primarily seek to satisfy the desire that gave it birth. The whole energy of this love is directed towards the intelligible reality seen in a flesh, not to be attained in the flesh. What is called "Greek love" is only a matter to be shaped, a force to be made use of. This is why, as we shall see, what flowed from it prefigured the "courtly love" of the Middle Ages. The lover pays homage to the beloved as to the source of his valor and his virtue. He "makes a god of him, raises a statue to him in his heart and adorns it richly for its worship and the solemnizing of its mysteries." Aware of the new qualities he owes to him, he loves him ever more deeply, and in absence lives upon his memory. Because he is a man he will be wrought upon by unclean longings, but after long and violent struggles his soul is able to follow the loved one "with respect and awe." And he who is loved, who at first rightly fears that he might be drawn into a shameful intercourse, ends by such a realization of what his lover needs of him that "at the appointed age and time he is led to receive him into his intimacy." Thus Petrarch as he grew old hoped to enjoy at last an intimate friendship with Laura. But even the hazardous experiments later to be codified by André le Chapelain are foreseen in *Phaedrus*.

Like the lover, "although less violently," the beloved on his side wants to see his lover, "touch him, kiss, embrace him, and probably not long afterwards his desire is accomplished. When they meet, the wanton steed of the lover has a word to say to the charioteer; he would like to have a little pleasure in return for many pains, but the wanton steed of the beloved says not a word, for he is bursting with passion which he understands not;—he throws his arms round the lover and embraces him as his dearest friend; and when they are side by side, he is not in a state in which he can refuse the lover anything, if he ask him; although his fellow steed and the charioteer oppose him with arguments of shame and reason."[2]

Such was the sword of division which King Mark was to see between Tristan and Iseult as they lay asleep in the forest of Morrois.

Man does not seem to have changed greatly in the narrow space of time in which we can observe him historically. There will always be people to whom such feelings are quite incomprehensible, and even a little ridiculous. Odd as it may seem, Chateaubriand is of their number, for he wrote from Avignon to Fontanes on November the 6th, 1802, "I am just back from Vaucluse and will tell you all about it. It is worthy of its fame. But Laura the prude and that bright person Petrarch quite spoilt the fountain for me." Vulgarity could hardly be more arrogant.

But when you read Plato you get, wrongly perhaps but irresistibly, the feeling of inversion reversed. Is he still talking of love at all? That is the whole problem, and it seems hopeless to solve it, you must simply take your choice. For those who experience such a passion it seems not merely to be love, but the only kind of love worthy of the name. Tell them that they are dreaming of love rather than living it, and you merely excite their contempt. And with good reason, for it is from a real passion they are suffering, it is with a real passion they are at strife, not to be rid of it

---

2. *Greek Literature in Translation*, p. 507 (Plato: *Phaedrus*).

but to aggravate it. Who says that Tristan and Iseult did not love? Both said so definitely that they did. Tristan says that if Iseult loves him, it is because of the love philtre: she replies, "Sire, by God most holy, he does not love me, nor I him, except through a herb wine of which I drank and he drank, and this was sin." In other words, they both clearly declare that they do love each other. There is a world of difference between saying that you do not love someone, and saying that you love him only because you cannot help it. Love sprang upon them of a sudden through no deliberate will of theirs. This is the rule of the *innamoramento*, which is only a part of the romantic stock-in-trade of every literature because it is a reality of every age. Make no mistake, the love of Dante for Beatrice, like the love of Petrarch for Laura, sprang up so strongly and rose so high only because an intense physical emotion was there to feed its roots. These are not loves of the mind alone but of the total human being.

The "Platonic" nature of these passions does not consist in the fact of their purity, nor even in a desire for it; even when the choice of purity is deliberate, it is never made as an end but as a means. If the artist refuses to satisfy his desires, it is solely on account of his art, for reasons unrelated to the moral law. He is concerned with what may be called the hygiene of creation. Like the philosopher Plato, although less lucidly, the artist sometimes interprets the physical as a concrete experience of the spiritual. Yet it is not as arising from the physical or beyond it, but within the physical, that he encounters spirit: there alone, instead of divining its presence or conceiving its nature in the abstract, he sees it and touches it. Why may not this occur in a human face or body? St. Augustine found, in the very act of carnal intercourse, the intelligible light of number. It is an absurd mistake to think Christianity utterly condemns sensual pleasure—to think, as some strangely do, that sensual delight is held by all theologians to be the result, culpable in its very nature, of original sin, if not that sin itself. Gregory of Nyssa did certainly hold the view that but for sin men would have multiplied like angels through the direct will of God. But the robust common sense of Thomas Aquinas would make no terms with such fancies. He thought that if God created the organs of reproduction, he did so for a purpose, and that what brings shame into the use of them today is the fact that we are no longer masters of our desires. Man, in short, need not blush for procreation, which belongs to his nature, but only for having become the slave of his own animality. The Angelic Doctor did not even allow that, for a man in the state of original innocence, the pleasure accompanying acts of intercourse would be less than in his fallen state. On the contrary, it would have been much greater, because nature would have been pure and the human body more sensitive. But for original sin man would have been continent, with a continence that would be no virtue since it would call for no effort. Always master of his desires, he would neither have to restrain them unreasonably, nor in using them have to feel self-reproach for enjoying their use. There is nothing the matter with nature except the disorder resulting from sin.

The persistent illusion of fallen man is therefore far from wholly false—the belief that sexual pleasure can reopen for him the gates of the earthly paradise. For indeed it ought to be able to open them. Man should be able without scruple to enjoy intellectual beauty enfolded within the physical, to look upon the most lovely face with admiration wholly free from craving. That this is not so, Plato reminds us clearly enough. Standing halfway between the philosopher and the man in the street—for his ideas are more concrete than the philosopher's, more abstract than the common man's—an artist feels the necessity of the incarnation in a living person of the ideal he is pursuing. He dreams of an impossible being, objectively real yet with all the purity of an abstraction. Not finding this being, he creates one of his fancy. Chateaubriand, for instance, did not waste his time touching up his "madames" to make them into Muses. The only Muse he had was his sylph who never existed at all.

The amorous experience of the artist, when it is not a mere commonplace love affair, is a mixture of eroticism and the quest for beauty. The Muse, every time that she appears, and in the degree to which she deserves the name, plays the uneasy role of revealer of the spirit through the flesh. At the beginning she has no personal significance. Plato observed, and the poets have repeated it a thousand times, that it is only little by little that she has any active part to play. At first all that is asked of her is to exist; yet at the same time she becomes, from the moment she is picked out, the center of a storm of feeling in which forces of which she is unaware go forth from her, beat upon the poet, and finally beat back upon herself in the form of his demands. The Muse does not always even share the desires she awakens, and the poet may be aware of this without ceasing to love her, may even indeed have no wish that she should share his craving. He wants from her a different kind of response, a communion of thought and feeling which enables him as artist to associate her with his work. If he does not ask her for a guiding idea, at least he expects to get from her the power to carry it out. Surprised and flattered by the agitation her presence awakens in the poet, the Muse is yet more thrilled at finding herself an object of worship, treated as a sort of divinity. The happiest of women is never so happy that she will not enjoy this extra portion of homage. The real danger for the Muse is not to realize that, even if it is all centerd on her, what is really happening in the poet's heart is a kind of sacred frenzy, of which she is not the cause but only the occasion.

The complex nature of this experience, sensual, aesthetic,

sometimes religious, makes it possible to explain it in three different ways—reducing it to a merely erotic emotion, keeping it on the level of art, or raising it to the higher level of religion. If one must simplify it, the only legitimate way is to keep it on the plane of art, for we find experiences of poets and painters which start from and return to their art so completely that they are wholly ordered towards this end and derive all their meaning from it. You will see why this interpretation seems to me the soundest, provided it is applied within limits and reckons with the unforeseeable complexity of reality. It is no affair of a mechanical arrangement set up in advance, only waiting for the poet's sensual emotion to release both his poetic inspiration and the desire to turn his Muse into a goddess. The experiences discussed will be individual, lived through by people so various and in such different circumstances that, even if one were in possession of all elements of the problem, it would be impossible to foretell how the romance would develop. Actually as one studies them one is struck by a twofold surprise—at seeing certain general rules constantly verified, yet verified in so original and unexpected a fashion that fidelity to them never becomes hackneyed. Then, too, not all these affairs develop to their conclusion. Some are, so to speak, archetypes, others mere sketches or attempts that have failed. I am very far from claiming to have found a set of rules or written an introduction to the history of Muses as such: such general principles as emerge from our study will be useful only if they are flexible enough to be applied to all these experiences without ignoring the many variations that make them so widely different from one another. Not only that: any given relationship is in a state of perpetual change, always on the point of melting into something else, or even ceasing altogether.

Everyone has, of course, a perfect right to interpret these stories in his own fashion. Let the psychologists, for instance, see in them case histories of eroticism or libido. They may not be precisely love stories, but there is an element of libido in all of them, and Freud deserves to be given a hearing, especially as, if he has oversimplified psychological reality, others have greatly oversimplified his teaching. Although he often allows himself to be led into oversimple formulas, he has not always maintained, as some accuse him of doing, that art is a direct transformation of libido. It would be true to say that according to Freud, the sublimation of sexual desire consists in attaching it to tendencies other than it. In the matter of Muses we are faced, it may be said, with a transference, quite classical in psychoanalysis, of libido itself directed towards art enjoyment. What would Beatrice have thought of the Muse of October who, to comfort her poet, finds it enough to say—"Have you not now a beautiful mistress?" How little de Musset knew himself. "I have the heart of Petrarch," he said, "but not his genius." Exactly the opposite is true. Where he failed, not indeed to be a poet, but to belong to the spiritual family of the greatest among them, was in seeking nowhere save in lust for the love which moves the spheres.

I am not criticizing him. It is only a matter of discriminating between the man who sang of his mistresses with as much talent as though they had been his Muses, and those whose genius wrought their Muses into their art and served them only in order to serve it the better. Their initial impulse is from art, not sex. Even when the discovery of the Muse seems a total surprise, as it was with Petrarch, one wonders whether he was not subconsciously looking for Laura. At least it is certain that once the affair has begun, it is Art which carries it on, to such a degree that the most clear-sighted of the artists, Baudelaire for instance, become fully aware that they are creating their Muse, and see themselves at work shaping her. This is not art grafted on sensuality, nor even sensuality grafted on art. The artist himself is the essence of the adventure, which is precisely the birth of a great work of art. The poet himself, in the concrete fact of his personality, must make himself into the man who can give birth to the work. This can only be through the exaltation of the love his Muse inspires in him, and he is right to call her his "Inspiration".

You can see the thing more clearly still if you compare the artist in love with the ordinary lover. Freud has well noted the inclination of the man who is wildly in love to immerse himself in the woman he loves: "The 'I' becomes less and less demanding, more and more humble, while the object of love becomes more and more splendid and valuable, drawing upon itself all the love the 'I' might feel for self. The natural consequence of this is often the complete sacrifice of the self. The object absorbs, as it were devours, the self." This is obviously true, but in the case of the artist it is true also that his "I" is absorbed by his work before the Muse gets at it, and his art will devour not only his "I" but hers as well. The Muse who believes herself to be the climax of the story is certain of bitter disappointment, for the ego drowning itself in the beloved drowns her too in itself. He absorbs his beloved even more completely than he lets himself be absorbed, for both are sacrificed to something quite other. The living incarnation of his creative longing, the Muse, is far less the woman than the artist; and, more even than the work he is going with her aid to create, she is his masterpiece. Of the two she is the harder to bring into being. With whatever docility and understanding sympathy she tries to play her part, she never becomes wholly what the artist wanted her to be. The foot of the woman always shows below the white robe of the Muse. And the artist is only too conscious of it!

Woman and Muse are inseparable, but they are identical only through the creative genius of the poet: the Muse is his shaping of the woman into the being of his dreams, ideal and yet also real, desirable, and inaccessible like the perfect beauty he seeks to create.

These stories cannot rightly be estimated in the terms used by a critic of today to sum up the investigations of psychologists into "the loves of the poets." "The result of these investigations is practically always the same: the artist's creative work springs from his sexual desires. The artist, an unhappy and frustrated being, transforms into the bitter sweet of his imaginative life the setbacks and disappointments of practical experience." This may be true to a certain degree about Alfred de Musset. But it must first be explained why frustrated desires, which are so very common, so seldom give birth to experiences, until at last, seeing what is left in their hands of all they thought to seize, they say, "Yet one more failure."

We men of today are not exempt from the same experience. Everything brings us back to the "promise that cannot be kept." In our own age the genius of Paul Claudel has only rediscovered and re-illumined this eternal truth—"Dear Rodriguez, I am powerless to keep the promise my body made you." Thus it is that according to Plotinus, Dante, Petrarch, Baudelaire, and so many others, always among the greatest, we may understand the role of the muse if we approach as philosophers the problem of its origin. But is it not better with such a question to let the experience of the artists themselves be our guide to the answer?

For those of us who know nothing about the artist's experience save what they have told us of it, wisdom lies in believing them, and in retracing with them the road they trod—inserting as little of our own as possible and never intentionally; listening closely in the hope of understanding a little, having no aim except to sketch the wealth of a kingdom whose gates we have only set ajar. And after all, it is better to gaze on the kingdom from a little distance, to respect the occasional disorder, than to throw it into real confusion by laying out broad straight avenues of our own.

II.   Petrarch and Laura

Francesco Petrarch saw Laura for the first time on the 6th of April, 1327, at the hour of Prime in the Church of St. Clare at Avignon, whither both had gone for their Holy Week devotions. Francesco was then in his twenty-third year. This worldly, elegant young clerk who never had received and never would receive even a minor ecclesiastical order, merely sought from the Church a career in which he could freely follow his passionate love of literature. We know nothing with certainty about the identity of her whom he called Laura, whether she was Laura de Noves, whether, as seems probable, her name was Laurette. Other things we do know, as we shall see, but her civil state remains a mystery. Was she still a girl or already married when Petrarch first looked upon her. There are arguments on both sides. The one thing certain is that she existed, that Petrarch saw her, and that this meeting of the 6th of April, 1327, left in his heart a thorn from which he suffered long.

This date seems as certain as any date in history can be, for Petrarch recalled it too often and too solemnly to leave us in any doubt. If he is deceiving us, it is because he himself was mistaken. However, there remains a difficulty despite all the efforts made to solve it. In the third sonnet of the *Canzoniere* the poet says that Laura took possession of his heart "the day that the sun's rays were darkened out of pity for their Creator." The reference is clearly to the story of the Passion: the day can only have been Good Friday. But the 6th of April, 1327, was Monday in Holy Week. Did Petrarch mix up these two days in his memory? It seems hard to believe but not impossible. Another poet certainly fell into an error of this kind, inversely, substituting an ordinary day for a dedicated one. We know that Victor Hugo and Juliette Drouet believed all their lives that the night of the 17th of February, 1833, when their love brought about—among other things—Juliette's moral transformation, was Shrove Tuesday, whereas it was actually the preceding Sunday. It may be that with both poets the power of suggestion and the symbolism of these days created the illusion. Or could Petrarch have substituted Friday for Monday simply for the poetic effect? This is not impossible, for he spoke only once of Good Friday and without giving a date, whereas he has several times mentioned the date without giving the day. Yet too it is possible that both are correct—even apart from the suggestion made by the Abbé de Sade that Petrarch had chosen to follow the Jewish Calendar! He may have first seen Laura on Monday the 6th of April, 1327, and, having experienced an emotion so strong as to long for its renewal, have returned to the same place to look for her four days later. Or perhaps he was not overcome at the first meeting but only on the following Friday. "This day did not seem to me among those when one is open to amorous adventure. I went along peaceful and relaxed. Thus my suffering came to birth in the midst of the world's sorrow." We can never really know.

At the very outset, then, every effort at an exact interpretation of the manuscripts is seen to be difficult. The *Canzoniere*, as it reached us, and that means as Petrarch chose that it should be, does not allow us to follow the story of his passion in detail. The prefatory sonnet itself explains this, for the parts are not put together in chronological order as they were written, but in view of the poetical effect. This collection of works of art is itself a work of art which the author (as we know) did not cease to retouch down to the end of his life. Add to this our ignorance of many historical details, the knowledge of which might affect our interpretation of the work to a degree that we cannot even imagine. The contempt of the pure aesthete for everything except the beauty of Art is perfectly legitimate, but so in its own order is the interest of the historian in whatever links the work to the man who made it: I do not despair of reconciling these two attitudes. How can we understand a work of art while neglecting all the light cast on it by history? Unfortunately in Petrarch's case the rays are sparsely measured to us. We all read the *Canzoniere* today like people reading Baudelaire's *Fleurs du Mal* knowing nothing of Jeanne Duval, Marie Daubrun or Madame Sabatier. That this is a good way for poets to read poetry I willingly grant. But it is not the best way for one who wants to detect the secret of a seeding of which nearly everything except the fruiting is lost. Certain critics think they have managed to prove that several parts of the *Canzoniere* were not even written for Laura. Their arguments appear actually far from conclusive. But if they were right, Petrarch's intention would be no less clear: even if he is in debt to other women, the poet is offering everything he has to Laura. He remembers her alone and plainly wishes us to remember no other woman. The *Canzoniere* is the poet's homage to the unique woman, to the Inspiration without a rival whom alone he desires to honor.

Petrarch anyhow gives us in his poetry enough definite indications to justify certain cautious theories about his love history. The poet speaks of his passion for Laura as of a sudden wound from which love came pouring out in all its strength, torrential, overwhelming. No refutation is possible, although this April love does seem a little too faithfully built on the rules of courtly poetry. Yet if so many poets do fall in love in the spring, it is perhaps because that season really helps love. An experience is nonetheless authentic because it has happened to many another. What seems more strange is that, from the very first poems of the *Canzoniere*, the present seems to have faded into the background and left the past to speak. I do not mean that the collection begins with poems that are retrospective (apart from the first) but that from the very beginning the story we are reading appears to be already ended. In vain may be sought anywhere in the book a lyric outburst of the youthful passion of a lover filled with the craving and the hopes that follow first meetings. It all reads as though Petrarch had tasted only the bitterness of his beautiful Laurel from the moment he began to make poetry of her. Laura, it would seem, had become at once and solely the woman seen for the first time during Holy Week, 1327. In one sense he never loved any other, but she belongs to the past and he is never to see her again. There was indeed a time when Petrarch's passion was still young, but there is nothing to show that it was then poetic. The passion we are listening to in the poems speaks with the voice of age; and, however lovely the language, its youth is wholly in the memory.

It must be admitted that this interpretation of the facts goes beyond what is psychologically probable. A. Mezières has skillfully stated the elements of a problem that no careful reader can miss. Was the source of Petrarch's inspiration his love simply, or his love grown desperate? The latter alternative matches the facts best. Abbé de Sade suggested long ago that Petrarch only began to sing of Laura on his return in 1330 from a journey which he had undertaken in the hope of a cure, but from which he returned more desperately in love than when he set out. It is an attractive hypothesis, but it seems not unlikely that in fact the poet's inspiration only began to flow in real abundance three or four years later still, towards 1334. It looks as though, after the dazzling effect of those first meetings, the months and the years etched in Petrarch's mind ever more profoundly and totally the picture of Laura. The primary source of his poetry was less the love he had on that instant experienced than the fear that one day came to him— that loving her without hope he could yet never cease to love her. Certainly the dominant theme of the *Canzoniere* is Petrarch's love for Laura, but it is inseparable from another: anguish over the total gift of self that this love imposed, the revolt against an enslavement from which it would be heaven to be free. It looks as though Petrarch, too inexperienced to see where his passion would lead, began by treating it as a game wonderful to play but not stirring him to poetry; and became a poet only to sing at once his evil plight and his hopes of a final deliverance.

This makes it easier to understand why the first anniversary poem, dating exactly seven years after the first meeting with Laura, yet finds its place at the beginning of the collection. It is true, as we have already noted, that Petrarch did not classify his poems in the order in which he wrote them. All the same, all the items that are dated, without a single exception, follow a chronological order: and neither the tone nor the content of sonnets, songs, madrigals, or sextets gives any suggestion that they were written in a frenzy of new-born love. The poet's utterance seems rather that of a divided than of an impassioned heart.

What a strange collection is this incomparable *Canzoniere*!

The sonnet that introduces it announces that the story it tells is already at an end. A weary Petrarch gazes from the heights of his glorious old age upon all these masterpieces that will forever bear witness to his folly as well as to his genius. Laura's lover, so long a legend to the contemporaries of his youth, now seems even in his own eyes just a little absurd. What a lot of fuss about so little! He cannot quite recognize himself in the man of endless sighs, the victim of a passion which—as only those who have experienced it know—is a matter more for pity than for pardon, but of which he is ashamed. And then he is lost in his crowding memories: the first onset of the love that would soon be his conqueror; praises of that land, blest above all others, where heaven had given Laura birth. Laura, the matchless woman whom his longings pursue but who will not even consent to meet his eyes. From this moment the poet dwells unceasingly on two main themes, which alternate or weave into one another: Laura is for him the straight road leading to the supreme Good; but though he is sure to reach this Good through her, he will never win the woman herself by whom he comes there.

Themes hammered out, you say, a hundred times, before ever Petrarch wrote. It may be so, but in him they strike a fresh note, rising from a deeper depth than poetic convention or even than Art itself. It is meaningless to say that the artist is here inspired by a vague Platonism, for even if this were true, how explain the Platonic inspiration unless by the abiding nature of a spiritual experience, an experience that recurs again and again down the centuries, an experience that no repetition can stale? In the tenth sonnet we meet for the first time, and in one of its most perfect forms, his treasurable confession, "I bless the time, the place, the hour when my eyes were lifted up on high and when I said, 'Soul, you should give thanks at being judged worthy of such great honor. From Her arises that loving desire which, if

it be followed, will lead you to the supreme good through contempt of the things men crave."'

A double error is possible here: we must neither overweight
these words nor yet see in them mere empty formulas. We have
not a philosophic doctrine here, not a religious belief either, but
supremely not a freshly desire craving satisfaction. Something
else is in question—that something is a genuine spiritual experience which we have no right to make light of. A woman's face
was enough to inspire the poet with contempt for the lower joys
to which men—and the poet himself insofar as he is a man—
are commonly attached. What says morality about this liberat-
ing emotion? It ennobles the poet only by directing him beyond
itself, as well as beyond all else, towards an Absolute, called by
him the good because it is henceforward the supremely desirable.
That he can only reach it through Laura makes her worthy of his
worship, but can this worship fail to lift him to heights where
she must become inaccessible? Petrarch does not fear, he knows,
that henceforward this is true for him—and whence comes this
certitude unless from a hidden acceptance of what he recognizes,
if not as his task, at any rate as his destiny? Not only is the woman
he loves in fact not for him, but it is of the very essence of his love
that she cannot be for him. For this very reason one asks, when
Petrarch uses it of Laura, what exact meaning the verb "to love"
has for him.

One hardly dares to ask this question, though it cannot
remain unasked, because it is so difficult to answer it without
some slight pedantry that may provoke a smile. What place has
analysis when we are reading poetic confidences where the sincere is difficult to distinguish from the conventional because
often borrowing its language, where one theme is constantly
exchanged for another or even interwoven with it? Petrarch is a
man of passion, devoured by most sensual love, a Christian who

knows he is a sinner and fights heroically against his passion, an artist aware of having found in that passion the very well-spring of his art. And he is all these simultaneously, lacking strength to enter upon the road he ought to tread—not that he does not know which road it is, but that his divided will dare not choose between two beatitudes equally longed for, but mutually exclusive, that of the artist and that of the man. The Christian in him has always condemned the sinner, but he knew that by many a secret thread the disorders of his private life clung to his love of Laura. It would all have been so simple if he could have got loose from his love, without drying up with the same stroke the source of another good, no less dear to the heart of a poet than is virtue to the heart of a Christian, the well-spring of his art.

The carnal nature of the passion he feels for Laura is one of its qualities most emphasized by Petrarch. Many people insist on finding in what he says of this nothing beyond a too familiar literary device. Certainly I admit that with him, as with all poets, the part played by literary artifice must be taken into account, but after all some other device could well have served instead of this one. Petrarch might well have posed as the poet of ideal love, whose soul communes with the supreme good through the soul of his Muse, transcending and ignoring his body's clamor. He did not do this, he did exactly the opposite. Petrarch was a man passionately in love with the woman whom he christened Laura, and we do not have to take his word for it—too many facts are established to leave room for doubt.

Most certain of all, enough by itself to make doubt impossible, is the fact that while Laura never became the mistress of Petrarch he did have others who were merely substitutes for her, there to perform the lower functions which his Muse refused. The obscure eighteenth sonnet, one of the first of the collection, hints at a veiled fear confirmed by definite events in Petrarch's life. You do not love me, he says to Laura, but I love you and I can love no other. If I banish my heart, and it vainly seeks refuge with you to solace its exile: "it knows not how to exist in solitude, or how to answer the call of any other heart. It may lose the right road, which would mean deep sin for us both, but all the worse for you because my love for you is greater, because I love you more." What can this threat mean except that Petrarch's love for Laura, ideal though it be in some aspects, has let loose in him storms of a sensuality hitherto obedient to the reins of reason. He admitted this later in the document entitled *My Secret*, which is of the greatest value to us today. It is a dialogue between St. Augustine and himself, with Truth as the arbitrator. Augustine, the very voice of his own conscience, calls upon Petrarch to admit that this pure and chaste love which the poet flatters himself he felt for Laura was no less sensual than passions of the sort commonly are. However skillful in debate (and he never admitted that everything in his passion was bad), Petrarch had to yield at last to the evidence, conquered by the very argument that is decisive for us today. It was from the moment in 1327 when his love for Laura was born that his dissolute life began. The evidence is all the more unshakable from the fact that it stands opposed to all those feelings cherished by the poet as most sacred and most dear.

"Yes, truly the time of meeting her and the time of my lost virtue are the same."

The mistresses who gave him two children, Giovanni and Francesca, make these words daylight clear: the love of Petrarch for Laura would not have started a moral crisis that was to last more than twenty years if it had been merely a question of an intellectual love. No passion can throw the senses into disorder in which the senses have not been already involved.

How about Laura? We have no letters or memoirs that enable

us to decide the exact nature of her feelings. It is at least certain that she let herself be loved. If Petrarch's ardors, poetical or otherwise, had annoyed her, nothing would have been easier than to put an end to them. The part of a Muse requires at least some assistance from the actress who accepts it. But in this case it seems especially vain to try for precision, if only because Laura's own feelings were doubtless badly mixed. Pleasure at being the theme of her poet's song, admiration, friendship, and perhaps more than friendship, were all seeking justification in the mission of his moral redemption which she certainly believed to be hers, Laura wanted to cure Petrarch of the wound she had involuntarily inflicted—but this does not wholly explain why she kept him in play so long with smiles and discreet encouragement, changing into the severity she deemed necessary every time the imprudently encouraged poet attempted to advance a step further. Of all the Muses we know, Laura will always be the model. For the very art of being a Muse is to nourish love in the poet, to let him realize that she loves him—that in fact she loves him much too well ever to grant him anything.

As I have said, Laura's identity is still unknown. There are, of course, plenty of people who know it quite well, but their conviction rests on no evidence at all. It would be a good idea if they could at least agree about a small number of established facts which are much more important than the knowledge of her name. Anyone may maintain that Petrarch's Laura was Laura de Noves, or if you prefer it, that she belonged to the family of Chabien d'Ancezune, Lords of Cabrières. But what should be no longer possible is to deny that Laura may have been Laura de Sades, on the ground that she was a married woman and the mother of many children. For it is absolutely certain that the Laura of the *Canzoniere* was a married woman and mother of a large family. It is no less certain that she was never Petrarch's mistress. If Laura had been an unmarried girl, he would have sung her praises, not in the Triumph of Chastity but in the Triumph of Virginity, and had she been his mistress, he would have sung them in neither. And there can be no doubt about her children, for Petrarch himself describes Laura as worn out by many pregnancies (*crebris partubus*). The fact must simply be admitted that Petrarch's Muse kept his love for over twenty years, in circumstances that might well have killed it, and even when he could no longer cling to the illusion that "the heavenly walk and exquisite grace of a being more angel than woman" had lost nothing of their splendor.

All the more reason, some will say, for concluding that Petrarch's love for Laura was no more than a literary fancy, or at most an imaginary infatuation which not even he took seriously. Certainly a literary fancy, for art as such implies some degree of fancy. But it would be a profound error to imagine that Petrarch loved Laura only with his mind—and it is most strange that the great historian of Italian literature, Francesco de Sanctis, should have fallen into it.

For Francesco de Sanctis, the fact that this love had no history makes it unreal. "It lasted," he says, "twenty years and was on the last day in exactly the same position as on the first, with no development, no succession of events." And why was it, continues the critic, that nothing ever happened? It was because Petrarch was a man without a will, and a man without a will is a man without a history. But on the other hand, even if it means that nothing happens, this perpetual wavering of a weak man is marvellously adapted to the creation of a poetic atmosphere. Whereupon, in a sally of somewhat coarse gusto, de Sanctis asks the reader to use his imagination on this Petrarch—petrified with love and incapable of making up his mind. A peasant would have said to him, with rough common sense: will you or won't you; yes, or no? If yes, be bold. If no, leave her alone. "Petrarch never crossed the Rubicon: his life was lived in a wavering imagination, never getting into action; anyone who knew him would say, 'the man was like the story.'"

It is true that this love never developed into a novel. If a novel means the story of a famous "affair," it is accurate to say that nothing happened. Petrarch did not carry Laura off; Laura's husband did not murder either Laura or Petrarch. But without being a novel, this love has a history, and if Francesco de Sanctis did not find it, it was because he looked for it in the wrong place. Petrarch himself did ask Laura, "Will you or won't you?" And she answered, "I won't."

It is difficult to understand how Petrarch's illustrious commentator can have failed to notice this, for to miss it is not to have read the *Secretum*. Petrarch did cross the Rubicon, but less lucky than Caesar, he found the opposite bank so strongly fortified that he had to cross back.

No doubt is possible here, for we have it from the poet himself, and a man is readier to boast of his conquests than to confess his defeats. Petrarch tried to seduce Laura and to make her his mistress, but he failed in the attempt. Far from yielding, she tried for as long as possible to cure his disorderly life, for which she was not responsible, even though the passion inspired by her had been its cause. The poet himself bears unanswerable testimony:

"She did all she could. And indeed, what else was her aim when, deaf to my prayer and unmoved by flattery, she kept her honor secure and unassailable, alike against my youth and her own, despite many circumstances that might have bent even a will of iron? But no, this great-souled woman recalled me to my duties as a man, and when at last she saw me rushing upon my doom she chose rather to give me up than to follow." These words are clear enough, and even if we do not know what "circumstances" were favorable to his passion, we do at least know that Petrarch was not satisfied with loving Laura with a love that dared not speak. If it had depended on him alone, this story of poetic love would have reached its climax in adultery—and what would poetry have gained from that? Laura found in virtue and reason the strength to make herself untouchable: and so we can glimpse her through the *Canzoniere*, skillfully nursing in the poet's heart the passion whence his songs flow; now she is full of severity, now she is friendly, playful, almost tender, accepting throughout the part given her by the poet, a part she could not have played if she had not accepted it.

No doubt the *Canzoniere* is literature, but in what way? Petrarch most certainly took his love seriously. When he became aware of his peril he began a determined fight, heroic if only because so long sustained, which he carried on until the late but complete victory won in ripe age. So little was this a literary amusement that the poet again and again took refuge in flight solely in the hope, as he says in the *Secretum*, of throwing off his sickness, only to realize that it was still upon him, right down to that day in April, 1348, when, far away from Laura, he learnt of her death. From 1333 to 1348 many anniversary poems inform the reader of the *Canzoniere* that the fight is still on: indeed a letter of 1336 to his friend Denys de Borgo san Sepolcro shows that his first longing for freedom began three years earlier, that is to say in 1333. This means that for six years Laura had ruled the heart of Petrarch without a rival, while another woman gave his body the satisfaction that she refused him. From this time forward landmarks are to be found, sometimes at lengthy intervals, but in quite regular chronological order.

In the second *Sestina* Petrarch is shown still loving Laura, but hopelessly:

"I fear my hair and face will both be changed, before those eyes are turned upon me of the idol I worship carved out of living laurel. For if I err not in my reckoning, seven years have now gone by while I wander sighing from shore to shore, night and day, through summer heat or snow." Seven years: this brings us to the 6th of April, 1334. Two years later in the same month comes the climb up Mount Ventoux made by Petrarch and his brother Gherardo, the description of which, although so stylized, deserves the fame that it still has. Coming down from the mountain, on the peak of which he had re-read a passage of the *Confessions* of Saint Augustine, the poet longs so keenly to overcome his passion that he at first pretends to think that he has won his freedom. If not free, he at least craves freedom, and his passion shall no longer have undisputed dominance. "Where I loved I love no more. I lie, for I love still, but with shame and sadness. I love but I long not to love, I would fain hate."

Returning from the long journey which had taken him to Paris, Liège, Cologne, Aix la Chapelle, and Lyons, Petrarch left Avignon for Vaucluse, far enough away from Laura to avoid the daily sight of her, near enough to be able to reawaken when he chose the picture of his Inspiration. This is the period of *Canzone IV*, one of his most beautiful, which still holds all its power of evocation. It too can be dated, for he writes, "I have been in the throes of this craving almost ten years and cannot conceive who will set me free." Almost ten years: this means almost April, 1337: Petrarch still loves Laura, but with a heart increasingly disturbed and increasingly longing to be free.

Nor is the nature of the freedom he was seeking in doubt. He was suffering from a tormenting and hopeless longing and oppressed also by his disorderly life. In his *Epistle to Posterity* he has used words so free from overemphasis that it is impossible not to believe him. "To say that I have never been subject to my passions would be agreeable but untrue. What I can say with certainty is that while carried away by the heat of my youth and my temperament I always hated my shame from my heart."

This is very much what Baudelaire was later to write to Mme. Sabatier, and it is hard to think of the coincidence as accidental. But since any literary link here seems improbable, an explanation must be sought in the experience common to both poets. Neither Petrarch nor Baudelaire dignified these passions with the name of love. In the same passage in which he scourges their base nature Petrarch writes, "In my youth a vehement love brought suffering to me—but this love was noble and unique. The suffering would have been more prolonged had not cruel but saving death blown out the flame which was already beginning to burn less brightly."

It must be granted that this story is not a simple one, but we should respect its intricacy the more because therein lies its fascination: the poet loved one woman only, Laura: she was never his mistress, yet this unique and noble love threw him into excesses of passion of which we know not whether it was the cause, the occasion or merely the excuse. Petrarch himself declares that it was the cause: it is certain anyhow that he believed so.

Another year goes by, and another milestone, the beautiful Sonnet XL, is set up on the melancholy path. "My God, the year is ending, the eleventh year in which I hear this cruel yoke, all the heavier the more willingly it is borne. Have pity on my sinful martyrdom: bring back my wandering thoughts to a more worthy object, remind them that today you were nailed to the cross." The meaning is clear: the day of the crucifixion, eleven years after the first meeting of Petrarch and Laura, is Good Friday, the 10th of April, 1338. The poet is still in love with his Muse; years are passing, but nothing can lessen the violence of his love. Here is Sonnet LXXI: "I long to fly, but the rays of love burning in my mind shine so bright that in this fifteenth year they dazzle me more than on the first day."

Fifteen years! This brings us to 1342, and Petrarch not only believes that he still loves Laura, but declares that he loves her more than ever. Nor is this all: "The seventeenth year of longing has gone by, and I am drawing near my end. Yet it seems only yesterday my martyrdom began." This sonnet, No. LXXXII, brings us then to 1343. Petrarch is forty, what age is Laura? That we do not know, but Petrarch's private record *My Secret* gives some details on what she had become which are precise enough to convince us that age had not spared her loveliness.

One sentence in this dialogue exactly dates the third part. "It is now sixteen years," says Augustine to the poet, "that you have been fanning the flame of sinful pleasures": he is, then, writing in 1343; that is to say, five years before Laura's death. Petrarch without argument agrees with St. Augustine that the woman he loves is a mere mortal, but she is, he insists, a mortal on whose face shines the reflection of divine beauty. Of course she will die, indeed she has already been so ill that the poet had written a funeral ode for her as though she were already dead. But what he loves in her will never die, for he has always loved her body less than her soul, whose supernatural virtues show him how the denizens of heaven live.

The debate that follows between Augustine and Petrarch should be looked at closely, for it casts a vivid light on the heart of this obscure problem. Still the lover of Laura, Petrarch is at once near enough to a cure to deceive himself no longer about the true nature of his disease, and sick enough to feel the full strength of the good and sufficient reasons he has for not desiring a cure. The first of these, in one sense the only one, is that Augustine is mistaken in scourging as a vice Petrarch's love for Laura. It may possibly be one, the poet does finally admit this, but not without defending the love itself from the scourging which his conscience bids him accept. Here we arrive at the center of the drama being played in the poet's heart. He knows, he admits, all the harm done him by his love, but this is in his eyes countered by something else, which a duty no less imperious obliges him to recognize. Like morality and religion, art too has its rights. Tell the whole story, admit the sins it has caused, and the *Canzoniere* remains a thing of beauty. To whom but Laura does Petrarch owe the power of creating the beauty that shines from it, a beauty wholly of the spirit? As long as he can keep the question on this plane, the poet remains invulnerable to Augustine's darts. Whatever else he may yield to the voice of his conscience this certainty remains: a woman formerly young and fair, today virtuous still and admired by all, was enough by the mere sight of her to inspire him with a love that turned him into a poet. For he gave up the easy, sterile life of common men, he embraced the immense toil of the artist, not indeed without a secret hope of glory, but that glory would be Laura's as fully as his, the beauty of his work being a mere reflection of her beauty. Or to put it even more accurately: because the beauty of both alike is the beauty of Laura. What does Petrarch mean when he declares that "Laura's fame awakened in him the desire for glory"—except that he wanted to receive from Laura that incomparable beauty which won glory for her, to make of it material for the beauty of his art?

The love of the poet for his Muse is shown here as the living force whereby this change is wrought. This is its very essence, and Petrarch knows it so well that—on the eve of renouncing a love which he consents to renounce only because he knows by a thousand hidden signs it is in fact leaving him—he is bent upon offering to it the supreme homage that he owes. Whatever happens, Laura will always remain the woman who "bringing him forth from the common crowd and guiding his path, aroused his slumbering genius and drew his soul upwards from its sluggish torpor." There is his achievement to bear witness: Laura and Laura alone made Petrarch what he is, wherefore the passing years cannot lessen her in his eyes, cannot even really touch her. "I loved her," he at last agrees to admit, "with my body." But he adds, "I loved her body less than her soul." The best proof of which is that the older Laura grew physically, the more Petrarch loved her soul's beauty. He still loves her as much as ever, "although that beautiful body, worn out by many illnesses and frequent child-bearing, has lost much of its early power."

We may regret the loss of Simone Memmi's portrait of Laura young, but it is certainly best both for her sake and ours that we cannot see her as she was in 1343. However that may be, the very frankness of Petrarch's words helps us to pose the problem accurately. However fleshly such a love may be in its beginnings, it involves spiritual aspirations which, suspect at first, are justified by its long life. In this amazing fidelity Baudelaire saw one of the surest signs of genius. And doubtless it is manifest so triumphantly in the greatest men because its primary meaning is genius keeping faith with itself. Laura's face may have lost its beauty, but that beauty lives still in Petrarch, pure and inviolate as on that first day—for it is the beauty of the *Canzoniere* and lives with its immortality. Without doubt—and Petrarch knew it—Laura turned him away from God, bringing about unwittingly his moral shipwreck, or, in a more subtle way, by directing towards a creature the worship due to the Creator alone. And yet, when he has said all, Petrarch cannot stifle in his heart the opposite conviction, which he shares with other artists living very near our own time, "It is certain that she made me love God." The great artist is a saint in his own sphere, and this gives him a feeling that in seeking and drawing near to the beautiful he is also drawing near to God. But to think yourself a saint makes it supremely difficult to become one, and because it makes this mistake, artistic sanctity usually excludes the sanctity of religion.

All the saints are not in the calendar. Wretched like so many other men and for so long, leaving confessions to tell us of his misery, Petrarch ended in the peace of a heart given to God which is the sanctity of the needy in the spiritual life—but in 1343 this goal was still far away. Bound to Laura with a worship that took the place of religion, the poet is still hesitating to choose the Supreme Good. If he will not give up the love of this incomparable woman, it is because to achieve beauty through her is still in his eyes one of the surest roads to bring him to God.

But was it really the best? His pitiless self-examination in the third part of the *Secretum* no longer allowed him to believe this fully. Indeed it clearly proved the contrary, for a truly divine love could never have resulted even indirectly in the general debasement of life he is suffering from and which he ardently desires to set right. Never did a more violent conflict stir the heart of Petrarch. His brother Gherardo, always ahead of him during the ascent of Mount Ventoux, had just taken the swift shortcut leading straight to the summit: in April, 1343, he entered the Chartreuse of Montrieux. But Francesco still vacillates: "Here I am, alas, and I long to be elsewhere; I want to will more strongly, but I have no will left and I am doing all I can to make myself unable to do more. The fresh tears drawn from me by my past longings prove that I am still what I was and that despite my agitation I have not yet moved." Are the *Septem Psalmi Penitentiales* contemporary with the *Secretum* and with Sonnet LXXXII? Henry Cochin, one of Petrarch's most penetrating commentators, was disposed to think so, and he may have been right. However this may be, there can be no doubt that the sinner is haunted by terror of a relapse, and that the poet is at the height of a crisis. Sonnet LXXXIII bears witness that in 1345 this fear is still with him: "The heavens have completed seventeen yearly revolutions since I began to burn with a fire that I cannot put out…. Will the day ever come

when the expression of that land and lovely face will attract my
eyes only as much as I wish, as much as I ought to wish?"

Two years later Sonnet CLVIII once again repeats the same
plaint: "After twenty years of harsh and dragging martyrdom I
have gathered no harvest but tears, sighs, and sorrow." We are
now in April, 1347, and we have only to listen to realize what is
Petrarch's state of mind: "Blessed in my dreams, content to pine,
to embrace shadows and chase the summer breeze, I am swim-
ming in a bottomless sea without a shore, I am building upon the
sand, I am writing upon the wind."

Unwise though it may be to spin theories out of the
Canzoniere, the sonnet for his twentieth anniversary must give
one pause, since it is enclosed with some formality between two
others which can hardly have been put there accidentally. One
of these sums up in a few lines the complete story of his internal
drama:

"Virtue, nobility, beauty, grace of movement, loveliness of
speech have seized me with exquisite tendrils, and the heart
rejoices to be held by them. In the year 1327 at the hour of Prime
precisely, on the sixth day of April, I entered a maze to which I
see no issue."

The second of these sonnets is, on the other hand, a poem
of worship, more free from grief than any other addressed by
the poet to his muse. To translate this either in accurate prose or
mediocre poetry is like a betrayal, but the former is the less bad.
Every word in this poem has its weight, for each one points to
one of the characteristics, at once physical and spiritual, which
together paint the picture of his beloved, not perhaps as she
appeared in her own or her husband's eyes, but as she was for
Petrarch. And this is the only Laura that matters to us, since she
alone was his Muse.

"Graces that Heaven though generous gives to few, rare

virtue above humanity, a mind already ripe beneath golden hair, high and divine beauty in a lowly woman: unique, unparalleled charm, a song that goes deep into the heart, a heavenly walk, an ardent soul that breaks through opposition and puts down the mighty, eyes before whose brightness my heart bows, a brightness that can light up the night or the deep abyss, can tear the soul from its body and give it to another: words full of exquisite or profound thoughts broken by soft sighs: such is the magic that transforms me."

For better and for worse, Petrarch had through Laura become another man from what he was before his vision of her: this he never doubted, this he repeated endlessly. And this, despite his scruples, despite his final Christian repentance, the poet could never perhaps wholly regret. Anyhow it was now too late, for the harm was done and deliverance was at hand. After twenty-one years of struggle Petrarch's human love for Laura would die with her on the 6th of April, 1348.

But was she really dead, and did his love for her ever really come to an end? The magnificent series of sonnets on the dead Laura make this doubtful. To the hour of his own death Petrarch never lost in spirit the glowing vision that came first of all and was perhaps the only one that counted, for it was from it that first flowed the inexhaustible spring of his song.

"She comes into my mind again, or rather she is ever there, for I could never forget her, as first I saw her in the flower of her youth, illumined by rays from the planet Venus. When I find her again, lovely and pure, withdrawn and solitary, I cry out, 'It is indeed my love. She lives still.' And I beg of her an alms, some words of her dear voice. Sometimes she answers, sometimes she is silent. And then like a wanderer getting back onto his road I say to my soul, 'You err, for well you know that in 1348 on the sixth day of April, at the hour of Prime, this blessed soul departed from her body.'"

There can be no doubt, Petrarch loves Laura still, but with a different and a better love than of old. The love that had transformed him he could not at first have experienced apart from the violent passion that was fused with it. Time had already begun to purify this love even before Laura's death, and thereafter he could hold it in its perfect and essential purity finally fulfilled. Yet we must not imagine that this love had become merely the love of an image, an idea, or a dream.

It is the woman herself still living whom the poet loves and sings. Petrarch had known for a long time the value of separation, which makes love fully aware of itself by setting it free from the daily round. He was at Verona, far away from Laura, when the news of her death reached him. He opened his beloved copy of Virgil and wrote upon the fly-leaf that moving memorial we know so well. Whence this sudden flood of feeling—for he was already apart from her and had no certainty of ever seeing her again? It was simply Petrarch's realization that death is not merely a longer separation but something altogether different. Like so many men before and since, he had experienced the total and sudden absorption of the one who lives by the one who has just gone. It is a presence lived all the more intensely, a reality all the more overwhelming because utterly unexpected: the soul of it is love and its physical form is grief. These are no metaphors. Petrarch knew this bittersweet experience, for the hope of once more seeing the beloved is sweet, but how great the pain of loss. How total the difference between a world which still held her even when unseen and a world in which the poet would henceforth feel unceasingly, "She is there no longer." However gentle this purifying death, it had come too soon and had broken a love which was transforming itself into a most pure friendship. "It would not have been long: the weight of years, hair grown white, brought

40

with them other changes: soon there would have been no harm in talking with her about my suffering. With what sinless sighs I could now have spoken of those long years of torture which today she beholds from heaven. I know this well and that she shares my regrets."

Petrarch seems to be committing himself rather confidently at this point, for he is no longer speaking for himself alone, but in Laura's name also. And certain though we may be that he loved Laura, it is much less sure that Laura loved him. In what way she loved him, if love him she did, only the story of Laura and Petrarch could reveal, and it is by no means certain that this is the same story as Petrarch and Laura's. What is quite certain is that the amazing vitality of the poet's love for his Muse is due to the fact that from its very birth it was set free from Time. Petrarch was, of course, unwaveringly faithful to his love, but the only Laura he loved was the girl he saw first in her youth, whom he loved still in the woman worn out by age and sickness who outlived her: Re-read only that sad sonnet, No. LXI, written when Laura's beauty was beginning to fade. Where are the golden locks scattered by the wind and the eyes full of a fire "that today is so lacking"? All that is in the past, but the lovely glow of the first vision is still intact, and after so many years the poet's love still lives upon it: "A heavenly spirit, a living sun I saw, and even though today all that is changed, a slackened bow does not cure the wound it inflicted."

Is Petrarch here showing a characteristic irony? Nothing of the kind. It is rather the exquisite accuracy of his words we must admire, for their precision is too cruel not to have been calculated. The urge felt by certain great poets to keep faith will never be better expressed. Laura as he will see her henceforward would be quite unable to pierce him with a new wound, yet she alone can bring back the pain of the first, which she alone inflicted. It matters little, then, if Laura changes as she lives on. The fidelity sworn by the poet is out of reach of Time, and its destructiveness for its object is enthroned in a past that he cannot touch. When Laura died Petrarch lost the woman who alone could bring back to him her whom he had loved since the 6th of April, 1327; and whom since that day Laura had merely outlived. Yet she could never die so long as Petrarch lived.

Any psychology which is not that of the poet is in danger of going wrong at this point. The feelings concerned are not merely different from other men's because more complex, but because of their actual function in the preparation for a work of art. And, bearing in mind what art means to the artist, nobody will be surprised at his using quasi-religious terms in speaking of his Inspiration. The origin of what is most divine for him must itself be divine. If there is only one being in the world who can enable his genius to fructify, the poet can only regard that being as divine. Lamartine was not mistaken when he discerned in Petrarch a devotion to beauty "almost as pure as a devotion to holiness." His mistake lay in drawing the conclusion that in her poet's eyes Laura was not a woman. The Muse is precisely the woman through whom is revealed a beauty which transcends her and which the artist serves through his art with completely religious devotion.

A rapid glance through the *Canzoniere* would convince one of this, but it is only through Petrarch's own view of his own story that it is possible to understand the poet's feelings. This view is made very clear in the words he puts into the mouth of Love in lines 88–90 of *Canzone VII* on the death of Laura: "If he has won some degree of fame it is through me alone, for I raised up his spirit to a height he could never have reached of himself."

Laura had made a great poet out of a little clerk absorbed in his Latin. Petrarch at least is convinced of this, and as he never

42

asks whether his own genius may, after all, have created Laura, it would be very ungracious of us to ask it in his name. "If beautiful things have come forth from me," he says elsewhere, "the seeds were sown by you."

Never does a flash of doubt come from the poet: Songs VI, VII, and VIII on Laura's life make up a trilogy which can have only one meaning: love is drawing from his heart "words and deeds which will, I trust, make me immortal, even if I should die in bringing them forth."

Fate has chosen for him this great good. No other road will take him so straight to heaven as his love for Laura, and none could sail on a safer ship towards beatitude. But beatitude means apparently that state of poetic grace of which Laura is sole origin. Blessed, then, be all things which brought him this grace: the day, the month, the year, the season, the hour and the minute, the lovely countryside and the very spot where he first saw the eyes of his beloved, the emotion of that first love, the bow and arrows that wounded him, nay the very wounds they made. But this is not all.

"Blessed be all my poems written in praise of my Lady's name, all my sighs, my tears, my longings, blessed the paper on which I won glory for her, blessed my thoughts where she reigns alone and no other finds place." The depths of his thoughts are clear enough and are uttered in Sonnet CLII, where the poet asks what could bring him consolation for the time lived before Laura's birth and after her death. Nothing (he answers), for through her he became Petrarch—or rather, it is through her he will endeavour to go on achieving himself. "Drive on towards heaven, my weary heart, through the mists of her sweet scorn, follow the noble outline of her steps and the divine beacon of her eyes."

Just a lot of literature, some will still say. Literature certainly, and the best, which is why we are still reading Petrarch, but neither the worn-out recipes of the troubadours which he inherited, nor his feeble attempts to lift Laura onto the cosmic plane to which Dante raised Beatrice, nor the vague neo-platonic religiosity inspired by his cult of the beautiful, destroy the fact that an authentic and sincere human experience is the real source of his work. It is true that that experience is itself a part of the work, for the "Laura myth" is a creation of the poet's in the same sense as the *Canzoniere* inspired by it, but this does not in any way diminish the authenticity of the experience. That the ideal copy of Laura should be a subjective creation of Petrarch's matters little: for this copy being to him the most objective of realities, the work whose birth it is to help is now certain to be brought into the world. And if the empiricism of the psychologist is satisfied by this answer, the metaphysician remains free to ask another—the answer to which he will probably keep in his secret soul. Is it, after all, quite certain that the copy of Laura is the wholly subjective creation of her poet? Is it even certain that between the woman called Laura by Petrarch and the Muse that he made of her, Muse and not woman may have been the real reality?

III. Baudelaire and the Muse

Baudelaire is not one of those poets whose name, like Dante's or Petrarch's, is linked in our minds with that of a single Inspiration. There was no lack of women in his life but, although his art gained something from each one of them, none, probably least of all his dark-skinned Venus, wielded over his work the sovereign power of a Beatrice or a Laura. With Baudelaire one finds not so much a Muse as the small change of the Muse he was vainly seeking. For there is no doubt at all that he consciously and determinedly persisted in the search, and this desire should rivet our attention more especially because it is closely tied in with the fashion after which Baudelaire conceived his art.

If this poet's search for a Muse ended in failure, the failure was not total, and his lack of success had its compensation in the amazing lucidity of the witness he ceased not to bear of his own experiences. In this respect Baudelaire would be irreplaceable—had we not also had Richard Wagner. These men are not explained by their great predecessors: it is truer to say that, by the light of their confessions, we can spell out the story of Petrarch or of Dante. Nearer to us in time they have, besides their works, left behind them intimate letters, letters in which the torments of their unquiet hearts are described with a frankness very rare in classical manuscripts.

Let us question them as to what they expected from the Muse they longed for. Men must have changed greatly since the four-teenth century if the psychology of the modern poet has nothing to reveal to us about the mediaeval poet. Anyhow, re-reading Baudelaire is always a pleasure, and as poetry is here in question the pleasure is also profitable.

Setting aside his "sick Muse," his "mercenary Muse"—and others of like kind whom Baudelaire himself did not consider true Muses—let us turn at once to his incomparable letter to an unknown woman. Some believe, I think mistakenly, that she was Marie Brunaud, who under her stage name Marie Daubrun was "the lovely witch" of *L'Irréparable*, and from whom the poet at one time hoped for far more than aid to stifle the remorse of a soul "swallowed up by anguish." Théodore de Bainville loved her too, and at one time was at odds with Baudelaire through a jealousy that was really pointless, and would still have been so had Baudelaire won from her the little which in the end was all he hoped for and which in fact he never did win. Supposing Marie really was this woman, Bainville was a hundred miles from imagining what were the real feelings of his strange rival. Today we still find them hard enough to disentangle.

What exactly was the story? Baudelaire seems to have solic-ited her while she was posing for some artist or other, where-upon she declared she would not return. The poet experienced "a strange melancholy" upon learning that he had, unwittingly, brought her to this decision; he was startled by a new feeling that stirred within him. Baudelaire had told this young woman that he loved her, and she had answered that she loved another, one man alone, and that any further suitor would receive from her nothing but indifference or even contempt. Whereupon the poet's instant reply was that he would gladly be content with the crumbs from her table. After this supremely commonplace scene, however, his imagination went strangely to work: as he thought about it he despised himself, and Marie's refusal changed what had begun as quite commonplace lust into love.

To answer the question what is the difference between lust and love, a complete reading of this long letter is essential. Every word in it invites comment. Despite the extreme difficulty felt by Baudelaire in expressing himself, we may also get from it certain indications of what happened.

To begin with, the poet has clearly taken a decision, the decision to make a choice, and in announcing that choice he sees it as irrevocable. "I have resolved to give myself to you forever." Why? Because their conversation had left him in a "new state," a state he is trying to describe. Ever since she had told him that she did not and never would love him because she loved another, Marie became "no longer merely the woman I want but a woman whom I love for her frankness, her passion, her freshness, her youth, and her folly." She has become beloved instead of merely lusted after, not because she loves him and he requites her love, but on the contrary because of the passion inspired in her by another. This paradox would make everything incomprehensible, if it did not actually provide the solution of a problem always presented by a feeling of this kind to the outside observer.

Little as the poet may have realized it, what now increases his longing, and may even transform it into love, is respect. Indubitably the passion felt by Marie for another man separates her completely from Baudelaire, but it adorns her also with a remoteness well fitted to exalt the imagination of a poet. Baudelaire now really wants to maintain an obstacle—to overthrow it by gratifying his desires would destroy his love. He tells us so in words that could hardly be clearer: "My loss is great since you have told me all: your decision was so clear that I instantly submitted. But you, Madame, have gained greatly in stature: you have inspired in me deep respect and honor. Remain always as you are now, and cling to that noble love which makes you so beautiful and so happy."

The element which from its very birth gives to a love of this kind a special character is here plainly visible. Baudelaire was certainly not the first suitor she had dismissed, nor was this probably his first experience. But he did not, like so many others, say to himself, "Lose one and find two." No doubt he had often talked like that in similar circumstances—but not today. Nor did he change into one of those trembling lovers who breathe out their sighs for twenty years, hoping that what has been refused today will at last be granted. Like the hero of *Portrait dans un Miroir* these men risk the discovery that what in the end they win is only a reflection of reality, that what they at last possess is not the thing they loved. Baudelaire is doing something very different: harshly dismissed by a woman, he grasps at the refusal that separates them and entreats her passionately to persevere in it. By thus entrusting to her keeping the "No" which transfigures her in his eyes, he shows surely his fear of a great loss if through kindness or weariness she allowed her "No" to weaken into "Yes."

What had he to lose? It is not to be believed that the poet renounces longing as well as possession. Indeed we can refine further and say that if we define desire as a will to achieve an object, the poet is hoping to keep the emotion whence desire is born, without keeping the desire to which it gives birth. To love without desiring is easier said than done. The man sees the beauty which the poet boasts of not desiring, and by this beauty he is moved. However chaste such love claims to be, the purity of an emotion is suspect in which the feelings, even if driven underground, are mixed with the most lucid acts of the reason. Exalted because inaccessible, the tangible cause of carnal emotion seems in some way to have become divine. Nothing is more striking in its repetition through the centuries than the tendency of such poets to talk the language of religion. Baudelaire is no exception: "You cannot halt my spirit as it hovers around your arms, your loving hands, your eyes in which your life dwells, your whole physical being. I know that this troubles you, but be at peace, you are the object of my worship, I could never defile you: I shall ever see you shining with the same brightness." It is the worship of a being of flesh, yet the poet adores this being as the pure source of his art.

All this combines to throw out our psychology, which loves to simplify everything and see it all clearly. Out of a passionate emotion that sprang from a chance meeting, the poet chooses to construct a spiritual quality so pure that it can outlive its cause: "I shall ever see you shining with the same brightness." Thus did the image of Laura, during the twenty years that followed their first meeting, remain in Petrarch's memory—as he saw her first at the hour of Prime in the Church of St. Clare at Avignon. What matter that she had since grown old and lost the flower of her beauty? The woman Petrarch never ceased to see, at whatever age she was, however old she became, remained always the only woman he had ever loved, the Laura of that first meeting, inseparable from the overwhelming emotion which on the 6th of April, 1327, turned the little clerk of Avignon into one of the most perfect love poets the world has ever known. This too is why, following Dante and Petrarch with a cliché which in poets of their quality must have come from some inner compulsion, Baudelaire places

ETIENNE GILSON

the source of his physical emotion in the most spiritual part of
the body: the eyes. He cannot help it. Once started on this path
he must grind out in his turn a theme of love poetry as well-worn
as the spring, the birds and the flowers, but like them permanent,
and commonplace simply because permanent. On this subject
the poet of the *Fleurs du Mal* thinks and speaks like the simplest
of novices. He has, in his turn, discovered that the power of the
woman he loves dwells in her eyes: he has told her so and he
repeats it: "You give me life and energy, not so much because
of your swift movements and the vehement side of your nature
as because of your eyes, which perforce inspire the poet with
an immortal love. I cannot express my love for your eyes, my
delight in your beauty. You have two sorts of grace, contradictory
yet harmonized in you: the child's and the woman's. Believe me
when I cry from the bottom of my heart: you are an adorable
being and I adore you."

Not a doubt of it! This river of clichés would be despairing
if it did not, despite its love-sick student style, give us so many
valuable pointers. Everything is there: the eternal permanence of
a first emotion that will outlast the years, the etherealizing of the
flesh into the pure spirituality of a glance, the device of the wom-
an-child painted of old in Dante's Beatrice, that little girl of nine
unassailably entrenched in the purity of her childhood, whose
first glance pierced the poet's heart with a wound never healed.
How many subtle tricks are used to assure the permanence of
these fruitful emotions. The poet hopes that the refusal of the
woman he loves will never be revoked, that he will always love
her in the shining memory of their first meeting; he reduces her
"adorable physical presence" to the pure spirituality of a glance;
he is attracted by a woman's grace, and claims to love her with
a stainless love which only the grace of childhood can inspire.
One can hardly miss the hidden desire of transfiguration that

determines these metamorphoses. What the body reveals to the poet is the soul, and what he asks of the flesh is spirit through the instrumentality of a beauty itself spiritual. Here we are back with Plotinus and Plato, or rather with that human experience which their doctrine did no more than embody in concepts: Aphrodite is beautiful because she shared in that intelligible beauty confusedly aimed at by lovers in their most passionate embraces.

Here again it is impossible to do without Baudelaire's own statement:

"I love you, Marie, I cannot deny it; but the love I feel for you is that of the Christian for his God. Never give an earthly, still less a shameful, name to this disembodied and mysterious worship, this chaste and tender affection which links my soul with yours despite your determination. It would be a sacrilege. I was dead and you brought me back to life. Oh, you know not all I owe you! From your angelic glance I have borrowed unknown joys, your eyes have given to my soul the most perfect, the most exquisite happiness. Henceforward you are my only queen, my passion, my beauty; you are the part of myself shaped by a spiritual essence. Through you, Marie, I shall become strong and great. Like Petrarch I shall immortalize my Laura. Be my guardian angel, my muse, my Madonna, and lead me on the road of Beauty."

On one of those days when the man and the artist reach the lowest point of their misery, Baudelaire had a chance meeting which his genius aspired to change from a mere unsuccessful amorous adventure into an inexhaustible source of poetic inspiration. What he wants Marie to be for him is precisely what Laura of old was for Petrarch. Neither Laura nor Marie, nor any other Muse, has any part in her election. Not only does the poet who chooses them ask nothing of them except to be, and to be what they are, but it does not even depend on them to be or not to be eternally chosen. Baudelaire explains this to Marie with a simplicity that is almost comic: "I will wait for years, and when you see yourself loved perseveringly, reverently, with utter unselfishness, you will remember how cruel you were in the beginning and you will admit how wrong this was. I am your prisoner: I must accept every blow inflicted by my idol. It pleased you to turn me away. It pleases me to adore you."

His idol! The tremendous word has been spoken, and it is indeed not merely one of the regular standbys of a poet's vocabulary, but also most weighted with exact and authentic meaning. Marie is neither woman nor goddess, she is a false god. In other words, she is one of those objects of worship which as we know very well we have ourselves created, and in which, unable to forget entirely to what degree their divinity is our own work, we never fully believe. In Petrarch's eyes also Laura was supremely an idol. And yet—and here we seem close to the most mysterious element in these adventures of the heart and of the artist—there is between the two stories a difference at once deep and subtle. Laura, as we know from Petrarch himself, always refused to be his mistress, but she certainly did not refuse to be his Inspiration, and that is why she was his inspiration. It certainly looks as though the woman he loves must at least play the part for which the poet has cast her. That part is doubly dangerous: she alone can keep alight in his heart a flame without which the masterpiece cannot be created, but if the flame catches her, it is quite certain to be extinguished. Laura managed to play the part faultlessly: for twenty years she cherished spiritual intimacy, safeguarding herself by such severity as necessary, and gaining for us the *Canzoniere.*

Baudelaire's admirers, on the other hand, owe precious little to Marie. Nothing could show us better how much the poet owes to his Muse, even if it matters little whom he chooses. For this time the marvelously clear-sighted Baudelaire deceived himself strangely. He believed that a Muse who refused to be a Muse was a possibility. Without a yielding of the spirit, however, the woman loved best and loved by the greatest of artists can hardly become his inspiration. Baudelaire at first thought he could without this: you do not love me but I love you: the point is of no importance. He was self-deceived, but perhaps he was in fact less convinced than he boasted, for in this really inexhaustible letter (we can never be grateful enough to Marie for keeping it) he does say, "Give me an answering word I entreat, I beg of you, just one word." This "token of friendship," this "glance" which the poet implores are small things enough, a bare minimum, but this minimum is a real necessity. Petrarch received it from Laura, she was really his Muse. Baudelaire did not receive it from Marie, and he knew it from the first that he never would: "if you only realized how much I love you. I throw myself at your feet: speak one word to me, only a single word.... No, you will never speak it."

Marie did not speak that word, and this is why she never became the Laura of this new Petrarch. The initial choice of a Muse is the sovereign decision of the poet and depends not at all on the woman he has chosen; but there is no such thing as a Muse in spite of herself. If he fails to win her consent, the artist can only submit: and this is what Baudelaire did. In spite of his oaths of eternal love, he neither "perseveringly loved" Marie, nor did he "wait for years" for a sigh from her in answer to his entreaties. In this very year, 1852, in which he swore an eternal love for the unwilling subject of his choice, Baudelaire replaced her by a willing candidate: too willing, indeed, to play for long the part of a Muse. But, as though this time he feared that the man might be sated at the expense of the poet, Baudelaire elected anonymity as a protection against the generous nature of Madame Sabatier.

What an odd business: this great artist, only just over the setback related above, sets out again to find himself a Muse. For he must have one at all costs. In a series of notes and letters of which every line and almost every word invite discussion, Baudelaire begins the siege of a citadel which he might have well feared to conquer too easily—so often had it previously fallen! It might be added that in yielding to others this lady had only been able to give them what they expected from her, which was something entirely different from what Baudelaire wanted. Just re-read that first anonymous letter which he begged her not to show anyone: "Deep feeling is modest and chooses concealment: the absence of a signature indicates a modesty that cannot be overcome. These verses were written in that dream state into which the image of their subject often casts the writer. He loves her keenly though he has never told her, and will have for her *forever* the tenderest feelings." Then follows the immortal poem, "*A celle qui est trop gaie*":

> *Ta tête, ton geste ton air*
> *Sont beaux comme un beau paysage*
> *Le rire joue en ton visage*
> *Comme un vent frais dans un ciel clair.*[1]

Let us not run the risk of psychoanalyzing, which would certainly prove a discouraging effort, but simply look at the envoi. The persistence of symptoms noted elsewhere is truly remarkable. This Baudelaire who hides his identity is no trembling lover, no gallant in search of a mistress, but a poet in search of a Muse. He does not desire Madame Sabatier, and if by the time she finally offered herself to him he still had not reached the stage of

---

1. Your head, your gestures, and your air / Are lovely as a landscape; smiles / Rimple upon your face at whiles / Like winds in the clear sky up there.

wanting her, it is in this fact that the reason lies hidden. From the very first Baudelaire wanted something from Apollonie Sabatier which would be lost by receiving her favors. What he expects to feel for her in the future he puts from the first into the past tense, as though the love she inspired escaped from the ordinary laws of time. As you listen to him speaking of this woman he has "keenly loved without telling her," whom he will love "forever," you realize that the poet has merely chosen a new Muse. The fidelity sworn by Baudelaire is all the more firmly granted, because it does not bind in any way the weakness of his body, for his body remains out of the picture.

From Versailles comes another poem on May 3, 1853, followed on the 9th by yet a third, and with it a line of excuse for "this idiotic anonymous versifying which must seem terribly childish." But what can be done about it? Our poet egoist is like a child or sick person. "When I suffer I think of those I love. My thoughts of you are usually in verse, and when the verses are completed I cannot resist my longing to show them to their object. And yet I hide myself like one terrified of being laughed at." Once again the excellent Baudelaire has said it all in four sentences, and no one could have said it better. He values above all things this woman of whom he thinks in verse, against those whose possible rebuff he protects himself by the ruse of anonymity, although he must in some fashion get in touch with her, that the spark may pass from her to him. In what transcendent sense is he an "egoist"? a little patience: he will soon tell us.

Meanwhile the letters continue to follow one another, becoming more and more urgent, and each one casting light on the obscure drama going on in the poet's heart. On February 7, 1854, he tells Madame Sabatier what he asks of her—which is simply to be there: "You do good without knowing it, even when you sleep, simply by being alive." But what good in particular?

"Imagine if you will that times, driven by some persistent torment, I find solace only in the pleasure of making verses for you, and that then I have to reconcile the innocent wish of showing them to you with the terrible fear of displeasing you. This is the explanation of my cowardice." But this man is not new to us who forgets his grief only in the pleasure of writing poetry for the beloved, and who loves namelessly to avoid either too generous a response to his love or the refusal of friendship. It was Dante who answered simply, when the friends of Beatrice asked him what happiness he found in loving her, "That of singing her praises."

It was the same with Baudelaire. After a night of joy and of misery the song inspired by the beloved image rises to his lips, purifies and redeems him. Even when he asks anxiously whether the women that poets love are befittingly "proud and happy in their beneficent work," that work still goes on. "I know not," he wrote on the 11th of February, 1854, "if the supreme delight will ever be granted me of revealing to you face to face all the power you have gained over me and the perpetual glow created in my mind by your image."

He had found the perfect description. All Baudelaire wanted was this creative "glow" to which he owes some of his finest poems, easily singled out by their especial beauty. We can well believe that no love was ever "more disinterested, more ideal, more utterly reverent." He asks of Madame Sabatier no more than the very least that love could ask. His abnegation as a man is complete: but not so his abnegation as a poet, and Baudelaire is too utterly clear-sighted to deceive himself about this. He does not lust after Madame Sabatier, he is even so little jealous of her lovers that he congratulates her as he did Marie on the excellence of her choice. All this means nothing to him, but he makes her serve him after his own fashion—though for a different end, and by a more noble service. Once again his own words must be quoted: "Finally, to explain my silence and my fervor, a fervor that is almost religious, I must tell you that when my being is overwhelmed by the darkness of its native evil and folly I dream deeply of you. From this thrilling and purifying reverie some blissful gift of fortune is usually born. You are for me not only the most attractive of women, but the best loved and most treasured of superstitions. I am an egoist and I make use of you."

Once again Baudelaire discourages the commentator—all one can do is to invite the reader to listen to him. Madame Sabatier is in Baudelaire's mind what he calls a superstition because she really owes to him the power to give him what he is asking of her. And he is so well aware of this that one might even query whether he possessed the minimum of honesty necessary for a poet bestowing a Muse on himself. How comment upon this letter which ends by his sending her what he calls contemptuously a "miserable scrap"? This "scrap" is in fact the sheerly lovely hymn whose music has sung in men's memories ever since:

> *A la très Chère, à la très belle*
> *Qui remplit mon coeur de clarté,*
> *A l'ange, à l'idole immortelle,*
> *Salut en l'inmortalité.*[2]

"Forgive me," the poet ends, "I ask nothing more of you." How right he was! But Madame Sabatier wanted to give him more, and that was what spoilt it all. The sequel is well known. In 1857 *Les Fleurs du Mal* was published—a collection whose title expresses perfectly the meaning of the whole story. Baudelaire sent Madame Sabatier a bound copy, thus officially bringing

---

2. To the dearest and loveliest one, / to her who fills my heart with light, / to the angel, to the deathless idol / greeting in immortality.

to an end an anonymity which had long worn rather thin. The Muse could no longer be ignorant what poet it was who had used her to serve his art. On the 18th August, 1857, plunged into a lawsuit, Baudelaire in the very letter telling her which poems were written for her, rages against "the wretches" appointed to judge him, for having dared to number among the incriminated poems two of those written for his beloved idol (*"Tout entière"* and *"A celle qui est trop gate"*). The magistrates were indeed wide of the mark. They fancied they had to do with an immoral poet who was admitting the public into his confidence about his pleasures—and the worst of it was, everybody else believed it too. But everybody was wrong, and it is best to accept Baudelaire literally when he tells us he was "struck dumb" by the young "sister" (or daughter?) of his idol, who asked him with a burst of laughter whether he was still "in love." He threw back the answer, proud, contemptuous and definite. "The common herd are lovers, poets are idolaters."

It was a splendid phrase, and anyone who still fails to understand him is inexcusable. The cult of the poet for his idol is not the ardor of the lover for his mistress. No, that sort of ardor, however elevated, is excluded by Baudelaire as the very opposite of poetic love. Of all places into which entry is denied it, there is none with threshold more jealously guarded than the domain of great art. For the man who sings of his passion and puts into verse elementary physical emotions, Baudelaire felt nothing but supreme contempt. He wrote to Ancelle on the 18th of February, 1866, "As to 'feelings,' 'hearts' and other feminine trash, remember Leconte de Lisle's profound remark, 'All elegiacs are contemptible.'" This was probably the deepest cause of his lively animosity against Alfred de Musset. One of Baudelaire's greatest glories is precisely that, at grips with a devouring sensuality, he not only never confused it with his art, but actually conceived of poetic creation as the true means within an artist's power of getting free from it. In a way he deceived himself, for he was asking of art what only religion can give, but the mistake was noble and certainly not total. It explains of what "idolatry" the poet is speaking, and why the more clearly he tries to see into himself, the more he conceives of the link between him and his Muse as a sort of religious and all-absorbing devotion.

"They tell," he writes, "of poets who all their lives fixed their eyes upon one beloved image. I believe indeed (but I am biased) that fidelity is one of the signs of genius. You are more than the beloved image of my dreams, you are a *superstition*."

This poet is certainly haunted by the memory of Dante and Petrarch, whose worship of a single goddess protected them gloriously against the temptation of the facile elegy. And yet it is the poverty of this greatness that an image by itself would not work the miracle. The woman must be as real as the emotion she stirs. In short, there must be love, through which, human though it be, the man who asks and the woman who gives are looking only for the birth of a masterpiece.

Baudelaire knew that Madame Sabatier might cause for him some anxiety. He took pains to keep her in her part in the act: the part of goddess—a role to which she was not at all suited. On the 18th of August, 1857, five years after his first anonymous letter, he wrote, "When I do something good I tell myself: here is something to bring me nearer to her *in spirit*." The italics in the quotations are always his, and no man has ever told a woman more clearly and more persistently, "I do not desire you." It is not surprising, then, that when the goddess came down of her own accord from the pedestal, which she had found extremely boring, her worshipper could not meet her desires by managing to treat her as an ordinary woman. The experts, of whom I am not one, disagree about what happened, the best-informed actually state that nothing happened at all. This is a possibility, although the famous letter of the 31st of August, 1857, could be interpreted in two ways. Anyhow, if nothing did happen that day, it was certainly because Baudelaire, far from ever desiring that anything should happen, had taken infinite precautions to prevent it.

What does Charles Morgan's Nigel say in similar circumstances?

For Baudelaire, too, it seemed a profanation and a sacrilege. If something did prevent his committing this sacrilege, the very opportunity affected him as though it were the act. A Muse who offered him something he could easily find elsewhere took from him in the same act what he could get from none but her: and he had bravely struggled to persuade himself, despite appearances, that she would help him to preserve this treasure in all its purity. Nor need we accuse him of too much simplicity. Nothing proves that this amiable woman lacked the capacity of justifying Baudelaire's ambitions for her: she had perhaps a vocation of which she was very nearly worthy. Anyhow, the next morning Baudelaire awoke with tortured nerves and "the inexplicable moral discomfort" that he had brought away from his lady's house the night before. It was less "inexplicable" that he supposed. On the 30th of August he had a Muse, on the 31st he had her no longer, and the prospect of having her henceforward as a mistress was very far from consoling him.

Lying before him were two letters in which she offered herself "quite shamelessly" not only in dreams but "body, spirit, and heart." How could she have known that it was the body that was *de trop*? Complete as her error was, it really was venial and Baudelaire alone was responsible. The poet had made a mistake when picking his Muse: in his calculations he had neglected an important element: if Laura had not the right to figure in a Triumph of Virginity she was quite in place in a Triumph of Chastity. Madame Sabatier had never made the smallest claim to a place in either one or the other, and Baudelaire could hardly blame her for playing badly a part for which he had cast her but which she had never wanted, to which she was not suited. All that he could really blame her for was that he had made a mistake about her which she certainly did nothing to cause.

This, with peculiarly masculine injustice, he did not fail to do. But there is some excuse for him: he now realized that Madame Sabatier could never give him what he hoped for: she was instead making promises she was incapable of keeping. He had vowed her an eternal love, and there had been nothing to stop his being eternally faithful, since the mutual love of poet and of Muse is made eternal by the very fact that bodily fidelity plays no part in it. But it was the improbable fidelity of her body that Madame Sabatier was now promising, and the poet did not hide the fact that he counted no more on her fidelity than on his own: "In short I have no *faith* in you; your soul is beautiful, but after all it is the soul of a woman." Which meant, no doubt, that she was more indulgent towards the pleasures of a libertine than awake to the ambitions of a poet.

He certainly does not sound enthusiastic: but there is worse to come. For poor Baudelaire seems so harassed and worried that the question arises whether he really wants the fidelity he dare not believe in. Listen to him weighing and measuring: "Look at the confusion the last few days have thrown us into." First there is the lawful incumbent, Mosselman, "a worthy fellow, lucky enough to be still in love"—they might sadly upset him. And then there is the fear that both must have felt of the storm they would provoke. They knew, Baudelaire especially, that "there are knots hard to untie." This lover certainly lacks enthusiasm, but it is the poet within him who is on the watch. The great and determining objection is stated nonetheless clearly from being stated last: "And then, a few days ago you were a goddess, helpful, beautiful, unattainable. Now you are only a woman."

How serenely cruel he is, how pitiless. Baudelaire does not yet know whether he has gained a mistress or for how long, but he knows very well that he has lost his Muse. His Inspiration is dead. She was his idol, but a profaned divinity is no longer sacred. She was his religion, but how can he go on believing when the unattainable ideal of which she was the symbol has turned into a reality of the most commonplace kind? "Never meet or never part" is the fine motto with which Madame Sabatier sealed her last letter. But did she really understand its solemnity? The "never meet" expresses the treason of his Inspiration, for "this positively means that it would have been much better never to have known one another, but that once together we should never part. Such a motto would be very funny on a letter of farewell."

This is really rather horrible, for the letter he is writing is actually the poet's farewell to the Muse he has just lost. Since we have come to know one another let us try never to part, but all the same it remains positively true "that it would be far better had we never met." However, the mischief is done. "Let what may happen, happen. I am a bit of a fatalist. But what I do know is that I have a horror of passion because I know it in all its falseness and the deeply loved image which has ruled over all my life's events is becoming too seductive." And one last touch towards the end of the letter, "Goodbye, my dear, dear beloved. I have rather a grudge against you for being too charming."

It would be an error surely to mistake for a man's physiological failure the psychological and moral recoil of a poet faced with such a lamentable conclusion of one of his finest artistic adventures. The reality is quite wretched enough without disparaging what are, after all, its noble elements. The type of love that his lady was generously offering was not what he needed to reach the high summits of poetry. Far from helping him, this storm of the senses could only hinder the one effort he had at heart, "that work through which a dream is turned into an artistic creation."

And this was something which Madame Sabatier cared nothing about, not because she lacked either heart or intellect but because she was totally unfamiliar with the problem with which Baudelaire was grappling. It is less surprising that she was lost in the maze than that in a confused sort of way she guessed its issue. Humiliated, wounded, frankly exasperated by Baudelaire's attitude, she did not see it as a physical weakness but as a refusal. This was certainly what enraged her and, after all, nobody can claim without absurdity to know better than she did what it was that really drove them apart. And when she tries to explain this sad affair, Madame Sabatier does not hesitate for a moment: "My anger was perfectly justified. What was I to think when I saw you running away from my caresses, except that you were dreaming about that other whose black soul and face had come between us?" Was she wrong? Most certainly, for it was her own soul, her own face as a radiant Muse that had come between her and her poet. Still her mistake was an intelligent one, for what she was offering to Baudelaire, Jeanne Duval was far better able to give him. She had not really the physique for the job of Baudelaire's mistress, but she did have for the job of his Muse—for that all she lacked was the soul. And so, offering the man the thing he did not want, she deprived the poet of the one thing he did.

It must be said in all fairness to her that she saw quite clearly what she should have been in order that her offer might be acceptable: you have only to read the unhappy letter she promptly posted to her poet: "Look, dear, shall I tell you my thought, a bitter thought and one that hurts me a lot? I think you do not love me." Nothing could have been more true, in the only meaning of the word love that she could understand. "You have no faith in me," she goes on, "but then you have no love. What answer can you give: is it not perfectly clear?" Alas, it was indeed. To the poet's appeal for the eternal feminine, the well-meaning woman replied by offering him Apollonie Sabatier.

This affair, which ended as a sheer misunderstanding on both sides, seems to have died quickly and left no great bitterness behind it. A note from Baudelaire less than a year later saluting his lady as a "very old pal"—or as a very old something a little less vulgar and a little more affectionate than a pal—gives us a pretty good idea of what happened. A Muse cannot become a pal, and this is why the small collection of poems written for Madame Sabatier received only one further addition.

This collection also stirs one's curiosity by appearing in *Les Fluers du Mal* as Petrarchian wedge of poems, but it would be an error to take for imitation what is in reality a fresh repetition of an old story. His moving *Confessions* strikes the clear note of an experience, at that date still unique for Baudelaire, of Madame Sabatier as a real woman and no muse:

> *Une fois, une seule, aimable et doucefemme, A mon*
> *bras, votre bras poli*
> *S'appuya...*

These lines express only pity for her whose "hard trade it was to be a beautiful woman; and for the plaint which she who was naturally "too gay" had that night let her lips utter: "a dreadful confidence whispered in the heart's confessional." But read again "*Tout entière,*" "*Que diras-tu ce soir,*" "*Le Flambeau vivant,*" "*Réversibilité,*" and there you will see the real woman transformed into the Muse, ideal object of the poet's worship, "Angel of happiness, joy, and light," "I am angel guardian, muse, Madonna,"

"Beloved goddess, pure and light-giving being," "Those eyes full of light lead me on." All these lines might have been written at Vaucluse: and if Baudelaire speaks of Apollouie Sabatier as Petrarch spoke of Laura, does it not mean that they both passed through the same experience? Nothing is more natural than that other verses written for Madame Sabatier should have been a straight borrowing from the prose of his letter to Marie. It has been claimed as a proof of the poet's "subjectivity," and in one sense this is true, for in these affairs his primary interest is always his art. But it might also be viewed as a proof of the exact opposite: what he had offered to Marie was the office of his Muse, and the titles of honor bestowed on her in advance, if she would but accept, were surely possessed of right by Madame Sabatier during the seven years in which she played the part. In this case Baudelaire is surely notable for a striking objectivity.

There is one especially curious poem in *Les Fleurs du Mal*: the "*Fransiscae meae laudes*." No commentator, to my knowledge, has identified its inspiration. Written in the language and the rhythm of a mediaeval liturgical sequence, it at once evokes the picture of a time when love readily took on the aspect of a religion. And it was certainly with this intention that the poet selected so unusual a form to hymn a learned and pious milliner: "Does not the reader feel, as I do, that the speech of Latin's last decadence—the dying breath of a strong man already transfigured and prepared for the life of the spirit—is of singular fitness to express passion as it is understood and felt by the world of modern poetry? Mysticism is the other pole of that magnet of which Catullus and his company of poets of animal union and bodily tension knew only the pole of sensuality?" Notice in the passage the barbed arrow loosed at the prince of Latin elegiac poets, and Baudelaire's own determination to lay under tribute the religious and spiritual outlook of the Middle Ages to find food for his art.

It is most important to notice how faithful Baudelaire was to this slight work. M. J. Moquet has pointed out that it is the only poem that finds a place in all three collections published by himself in 1857, 1861, and 1866. It certainly deserves this special affection, for even if it were less musically exquisite than in fact it is, it ought to be there. It is the perfect description of the ideal Muse as Baudelaire conceived her. Whatever may have been her real name, or even if she was nothing but the creation of his fancy, the Frances by whom his sins are forgiven, the divine vision that appears when storms of iniquity darken his path, who gives him back speech when his lips are sealed, is easily identified. She is the dream he has steadily pursued under the names of various women.

But where in truth did reality abide amid those earthly things whose existence he declared was of the slightest, or which, as he half believed, existed only in his dreams? To answer that, you must abandon art and turn to metaphysics. Baudelaire never did this, and when he does ask the question, the answer he half glimpses is not at all simple. The preface of *Paradis artificiels* certainly affirms *en passant* the existential primacy of the dream over reality, and this latent Platonism is one of the deepest and most abiding tendencies of his thought. But when he asks, in *Petits Poèmes en Prose*, "Which is real?" he is powerfully impressed by the tremendous complexity of the problem.

Both the Madame Sabatiers are real, but on different levels and in different ways. Both real, different from one another and yet the same: therein lies the mystery. The real Benedicta is indeed true sister of the eternal Beatrice, "in whom one breathed the air of the ideal, from whose eyes glowed out the longing for greatness, beauty, glory, and all the stuff of immortality." It sounds like a translation of Petrarch. Like Madame Sabatier and so many other Muses, this ideal girl was too beautiful to live long. She died and the poet buried her, "sealed in a coffin of scented wood, incorruptible as the treasure chests of the Indies," or in such treasure chests as the *Vita Nuova*, the *Canzoniere*, the *Fleurs du Mal*. The dead Beatrice, the dead Laura shine forth tranquilly from their tombs. Of different fashions and of a different era from Baudelaire's, these "wondrous women" did not in dying give birth to a vampire. No little creature was seen after the death of one of them, "singularly like the deceased," dancing frenziedly on her own tomb, exclaiming, with a burst of laughter, "I am the real Benedicta! Here I am, a nice sort of bitch! And in punishment for your folly and your blindness you shall love me as I really am."

As she really is: but what exactly is she? Thinking about one of the others—for Madame Sabatier's wholly poetic bitchery could only be that of a fallen Muse—Baudelaire could see all the more clearly that strange feminine polarity which was the continuing subject of his reflection. Because of it woman remained for him the most tempting of artificial paradises. How was it that this "most natural well-spring of the most natural pleasures" could pour into man's heart, along with its muddy stream, that pure essence which the poet's art alone can distill from it? But that is not the most surprising part of it. The strangest thing of all is that the poet, not content to syphon off the spiritual element from those disturbing emotions which pass from body to body, wants to seize upon it, to let it no longer belong to "the other" but himself try in some fashion to be transformed into it. Remember Baudelaire's profound remark to Marie, "You are the part of myself that a spiritual essence has shaped." It seems as though the poet could only become himself by absorbing the spiritual essence of a woman who, becoming part of the masterpiece as she is part of the poet, is henceforward a necessary condition of his work. The poet's love for the Muse is this very integration. The fact that this spiritual essence can be given only in a body is for them both a professional risk, but to reach the high peaks of art, risks must be run. This is suggested by the psychology of the great poets, endlessly haunted as they were by concern over "the eternal feminine."

This part played by the Muse in the lives of certain great artists recurs so regularly that its significance cannot be denied. No doubt there are women in the lives of all men, but even with creative artists they are not all Muses. Picture the *Divina Commedia* without the luminous grace brought to it by Beatrice: this is easy—for you have only to remember the *Inferno* and then imagine the *Purgatorio* and *Paradiso* as they might have been if the poet, grown old, had not treasured undiminished the passionate tenderness still awakened in him by the lovely face of a child seen in his far-off youth. This is a question of his art itself, of how his work would have been affected as poetry if he had not so deeply absorbed the femininity of Beatrice. Nothing could be more masculine than Dante's work, but the force of feeling that emerges results surely from the fact that, even on its highest and most desolate uplands, we breathe the atmosphere of that *Mundus Mulieribus* of which Baudelaire wrote, without which half of humanity would be absent and the masterpiece would leave our thirst unslaked. This woman's world is peopled indeed by bodies, and because he is a man the artist's first contact with it is through his own body. To join it in order to transcend it, at the constant risk of falling back into it, is the law of a relationship which might be considered the very type of a dangerous love affair if the reward were not sometimes so glorious. It is anyhow an enterprise upon which some of the greatest poets have embarked. These sentimental journeys of so well-defined an order are not mere novels but depend upon a philosophy of art.

To think of Petrarch as a courtly poet is an odd illusion—
even if in his bad moments he was just that. But try for a flash to
imagine what he would have been if the clerk of Avignon had not
met Laura! We should still have his *Africa*, which nobody reads,
and his *Letters*, which are almost impossible to read. Perhaps we
should even have the *Trionfi*, but most certainly not the absolute
perfection of the most beautiful poems of the *Canzoniere*. It is
the same with Baudelaire. He realized it, and the commonplaces
into which he falls in his hours of aridity are enough to show
us that he had good reason to be afraid. His descriptions in *Les
Paradis artificiels* and in a famous passage of the *Chagrins d'En-
fant* of the soft feminine atmosphere in which his youth was so
long immersed have a bearing quite different from mere anec-
dote. He is asking of the emotional disturbances, which he cannot lose without diminishing the artist within him, to introduce
into the sensual form the purity of the idea and this is the very
secret of great art. He has said it himself. Dante's youthful passion
for Beatrice still bathed with tenderness the most exalted of his
poems, and Baudelaire begs of Marie and of Madame Sabatier to
give to his work that "distinction of accent," or, more profoundly,
"that hermaphrodite quality without which the keenest and most
virile genius remains, in regard to the perfection of his art, an
incomplete being."

Certainly these second-class Muses were, even more than
Beatrice, false images of the good "who never fully keep their
promises." You must re-read "*La Beatrice*" to realize how this
poet suffered. Mocked as a fool by those for whom Madame
Sabatier served ends far other than the inspiration of a masterpiece, his real crucifixion was to witness the public prostitution
of a Muse—and the sun not halted in its course by the crime—
while she recked nothing of the eminence she refused, and of
which he had hoped to find her worthy. Yes, Baudelaire knew it

all, but as he roved after these empty idols he discovered some of his most lovely poems. And he knew that he could find them by no other path: "woman is inevitably suggestive, she lives with a life that is not her own, she lives spiritually in the imaginations haunted and fertilized by her."

These reflections must be halted on the threshold of a profound mystery. To create life, a man needs a woman. To create the perfection of beauty, it may be that the man must also be the woman. Here "to be" excludes "to have," which is doubtless why the great artist guards himself so zealously from enslavement to a sensual passion that drags down instead of ennobling. He cannot allow himself to be exploited by her whom he exploits to the point of being transformed into her to serve the ends of his art. The greater he is, the sooner he can dispense with her, but the nearer the work of which he dreams approaches the inaccessible summits of pure creation, the less he can do without her in its inception.

IV. Wagner and Mathilde

Like Baudelaire, Wagner is not associated in our minds with the name of one dominating Inspiration. Louis Barthou rightly headed his *Vie Amoureuse* of Wagner with the words written by the poet to Eliza Wille in a letter of the 30th of June, 1864: "I who idolize women." There is indeed a great deal about love in this book, but to think of Wagner as having had a "love life" running parallel with his "musical life" would be greatly to falsify the proportions. Granting, however, that there were in his life adventures explained by a more elementary psychology, there are others which will always remain inseparable from his art. Of none is this more true than of the episode to which we owe *Tristan*—unless, of course, it is to *Tristan* that we owe the episode.

Wagner's marriage with Minna Planer in 1836 had nothing to do with Muses. He married her, as he has told us, because a permanent union of this sort would guard him against irregularity of conduct and ensure the continuity of his artistic development!

In short, Wagner wanted henceforward a settled life, and we are
to understand this in a material sense as well as a moral, for he
was then, as he would almost always continue to be, overwhelmed
by debt! He always needed a woman to shelter him as much as
he needed a woman to be his Muse. She was sometimes the same
woman. He borrowed Otto Wesendonk's wife both to inspire him
and to finance the results of the inspiration. As for Minna, she long
remained a sure if stormy port of refuge, but he never asked her to
fertilize his genius. Fully conscious of the high destiny of the man
she had married, she served his air, with a devotion often admirable, by giving him some sort of home. Her defects, her faults even,
cannot be denied, but it was no easy task to be the wife of Wagner.
She carried it out, however, with no ambition to be anything else to
him, until the final crisis that drove them apart forever.

We need not linger on the musical comedy business of Jessie
Laussot, the young American wife of a Bordeaux wine merchant. You can read in Louis Balthou's delightful book how this
enterprise came to naught—as Wagner himself so pleasantly put
it—"in face of the happy issue of a treatment devised, by an experienced mother and a sensible husband, to cure the heart of an
inimitable passion." The Enemy of love had made use of everything in the fight, "education, happiness, conventions, business."
Jessie never dreamed of the perils from which her distressingly
normal husband had saved her.

Cast off and defeated, what an opportunity for Wagner to
turn Jessie into a Muse, to sigh after her for twenty years, to build
an imperishable monument of art to her name and the thought
seems even to have occurred to him. "Fare thee well," he wrote,
"beautiful one, holy one. You were supremely dear to me and I
never will forget you. Farewell." All this time Minna, worried but
patient, was waiting for him at Zurich, whither Wagner betook
himself to rejoin her.

It seems to have been here that in 1851 Wagner made the acquaintance of Otto Wesendonk, a rich businessman, devoted to the arts, and of his wife Mathilde, aged twenty, very friendly and a good musician. Obviously, what with the wife's charms and the husband's money, it was the ideal household. Art, of course, was all he had in mind: we must not imagine Wagner cold-bloodedly working out all the ways in which such a situation could be turned to his advantage, or even to the advantage of his music. Not calculation so much as a sort of animal instinct was continually bringing him into situations which he was amazed to find so helpful to his art! And if he did not plan the detail of events in advance, when they happened he knew well enough that he had expected them, wanted them, and, to an extent anyhow, helped to produce them.

The drawback to all these love affairs was certainly that Isolde generally belonged to some King Mark or other. This time the successor of the Bordeaux wine merchant was a partner in a New York silk firm. His more musical nature made Otto Wesendonk more vulnerable than Eugene Laussot. Against Wagner's genius he was as ill-equipped as Uncle Fulbelt against the learning of Abelard. He allowed Mathilde to take lessons from the Master, happy and flattered that she should be counted worthy of his instruction. And he had his own part to play: while Mathilde was learning counterpoint, he financed in 1853 three Wagner–Beethoven concerts. This won for him a little later the promise that his wife should learn one day to write operas "à la Wagner" with parts written for himself in English—for he too was a singer but in that language only. By now they were all friends together, in the unquiet intimacy that music generates— the delights of music are won only at the cost of a total self-surrender, and only in an atmosphere favorable to unconditional self-giving.

Who could resist the skilled handling of a Richard Wagner? That imperious genius lived only for his art, and the total sacrifice he had made of self gave him authority to sacrifice others to the same god. He meant just that by anyone "being his friend." You could serve him only by serving that in him which he served. Minna, Hans von Bülow, Franz Liszt, even Cosima, all had the same experience, but although they suffered, they all forgave him. In 1853 the Wesendonks were only on the outer edge of a whirlpool, and the movement that was sucking them in was still so slow that they were not conscious of it. Wagner must have made his first move on the 16th of March, for on the 17th he explains in a letter to Mathilde why in future his visits will be more widely spaced. "If I am more frequently absent henceforward—and how could it be otherwise after what happened yesterday?—rest assured that the chief reason is my desire to win your forgiveness by behaving better."[1]

And he sends her as a peace-offering some bars of a not very compromising polka. Mathilde is not yet Isolde. Wagner next pays an old debt to Wesendonk by sending his wife a sonata; he reads every morning a canto from Dante's *Inferno* the "terrors" of which dwell with him while he is writing the second act of the *Valkyrie*. And he turns over in his mind many schemes for new works, including an oratorio on Jesus. On the 11th of August he begs his "very dear friend" Mathilde to intercede on his behalf with the Bodmers that they should lease to him "for life" their property of Seefeld near Zurich: or if not for life, at least for ten years. True, this house is let already for the summer to a family called Trümpler, but as Wagner needs it the Bodmers

---

1. The quotations relating to this story are taken from *Richard Wagner to Mathilde Wesendonk, Journal and Letters, 1853–1871*, trans. William Ashton Ellis (London: H. Grevel & Co., 1905).

must simply cancel this lease. "The cleverest way," he wrote to Mathilde by Minna's advice, "to get at Madame Bodmer would be through vanity. Draw her attention to this fact: that it will certainly redound to their honor if their property is the worthy sanctuary for my future artistic creations." Minna was a good pupil in the art of enlarging on Wagnerian themes, but it seems strange that this warning was lost on the Wesendonks.

Time passes, visits are exchanged, and Mathilde, elevated to the rank of "very dear patroness of the arts," listens at her friend's house to the third act of the *Valkyrie*. We must acknowledge that if Wagner took on the grand scale, he knew also how to give. And now come some letters, unfortunately without dates, that strike a new note. "I am dreaming constantly of spending one short hour with you. My heart is very heavy—always occupied with the unique, the good, apart from which, poor me, this world holds no refuge. The unique good." Then this, which makes straight for our goal: "Will my dear Muse always be remote from me? I have been silently awaiting her visit. I did not want to plague her with my longing. For the Muse, like love, brings happiness only when she chooses. Woe to the fool, the man who loves not but wants to get by violence what can only be given freely. Nothing is achieved by violence. Isn't that true? Isn't that true? How could love be still a muse if it yielded to violence? But will my dear Muse never draw near to me?"

It could not be clearer. From 1853 to 1855, apart from forced absences for concerts, Wagner lived in a companionship, a sort of musical intimacy, with Mathilde which grew ever closer. What he composed in the morning he came in the evening to play to her, usually at dusk, between five and six. What musician could say no to such homage? Wagner found in her that delight, arising from contact with a loving and noble female character, of which he had formerly written to Liszt as being an "infinite good,"

which he longed for as a benediction on his work. Mathilde realized this and knew she was worthy of it. She was, then, really his
Muse even before he began *Tristan*, as early as the *Valkyrie*. But
kindly souls were beginning to take notice of his changing habits.
Minna was not the last to be distressed and anxious. There was
cause enough for worry, and only Otto Wesendonk appeared to
be unmoved. At his wife's request he bought a house near his own
and let it to the Wagners "for a rent," says Louis Barthou, "to be
paid mainly in music." This was in 1857, and Wagner was in the
seventh heaven. He began *Siegfried*, working at it joyfully up to
the day when he realized that life had just put him in exactly the
position of *Tristan*. He had read the story and already thought
of using it for an opera. Had life in fact placed him in this same
situation or had he engineered it for himself? We cannot tell, for
he did not know. On the one hand, he says frankly, "My poetic
conceptions always preceded my practical experiences to such
a point that I must account my moral development as wholly
resulting from them." And indeed it may well have been the
reading of Gottfried de Strasbourg's *Tristan* in 1854 that caused
his love for Mathilde to grow as it did. Yet on the other hand, as
he equally frankly recognizes, what happened to him was dis-
concerting. "You can easily imagine the profoundly strange position in which I now find myself as regards *Tristan*.... To ascertain
the propositions in which creative thought and experience at
first affect one another is so complex and delicate a matter that
a superficial examination would give only an incomplete and
distorted picture."[2] The idea here clearly inspires the experience,
and the experience in its turn feeds the idea. Thus the idea directs
the poet's life as well as his work: the world of experience comes

---

2   This quotation is taken from Guy de Portales' excellent book, *Wagner: Histoire d'un Artiste* (Paris: Gallimard, 1932), p. 244.

to him from within, while our world comes to us from outside.

Whichever way the thing went the musician's passion for Mathilde became so violent that it took all *Tristan* to sing it.

On the 21st of May, 1857, he is working at *Siegfried*, in July he announces that Tafner is still alive, but in September of the same year he sends Otto Wesendonk the following note: "Here, dear friend, is my rent for the first quarter. In time I hope to pay you the real rent, it may be quite soon: then you will cry out:

Behold my Lord Tristan
How well able to pay tribute."

It had been agreed that the rent was mainly to be paid in music, but Otto Wesendonk had hardly foreseen the particular tune to be offered for his entertainment. After this, things happened fast. The score of *Tristan* was swiftly completed. In October 1857, Wagner is asking to play Scene II of the first act to Mathilde. And in December, "The scene of the outburst between Tristan and Isolde could not be more successful. I am in ecstasies." The first three out of five *Wesendonk Lieder* are completed in the same month, and the two last bear the dates February the 21st and May the 21st, 1858. The state of exaltation in which Wagner lives his work while writing it reaches such a point that everything else, the so-called real world, seems to him now only a dream. He loves Mathilde, she loves him; she has told him so, she has told her husband and has ended by threatening to kill herself if he attempts any longer to claim his rights as a husband. To what an extent Tristan alone dominates the entire story can be seen in the homage Wagner pays to Mathilde on Saint Sylvester's Day, 1857, when sending her the rough draft of his first act:

All is blissful
Beyond pain's reach,
Free and pure,
Thine to eternity—
The anguish
And the renunciation
Of Tristan and Isolde.
Their tears, their kisses,
In music's sheer gold
I lay at thy feet,
That they may give praise to the angel,
Who has raised me so high.

In this total triumph of art, real life was so brutally ignored—for *Tristan* as he came to birth stifled in his embrace everything he could lay hold of—that its reaction was bound to be vigorous. Accustomed though she was to her fantastic husband's ways, Minna realized that this time there was real danger of losing him. Otto Wesendonk, even with the lava of this volcanic genius flooding over him, did not push his love of music to the point where he was willing to sacrifice his wife, the mother of his children, and his home itself. Wagner and Mathilde had to come to a decision—either do what Liszt and Marie d'Agoult had done or else separate.

They separated, and it would be highly interesting to fathom the meaning of a sacrifice the motives for which they had difficulty in explaining to themselves. Unfortunately we do not possess Mathilde's letter; but Wagner's answer, written on a Tuesday morning in the summer of 1858, reveals that a month earlier he had announced to Wesendonk his decision to break all personal contact with them. Having renounced Mathilde, he still did not feel "perfectly pure"—by which he meant: strong enough to persevere in his sacrifice if he continued to live close by: "I fully realized that only total separation or complete union could save our love from those terrible risks of propinquity to which it has been exposed of late."

True enough. If Tristan and Isolde had to face scenes with their respective spouses every time they went home, their love would lose a good deal of its poetry. It is clear that Wagner and Mathilde had no choice but to fly together or to fly from one another, but we should need a greater knowledge of their private life than we possess to determine why they felt they must make the second choice. Mathilde Wesendonk destroyed some important letters, as was her right—they were written to her! Wagner, also quite legitimately; has left certain indications which, since they have already been published, we can utilize without impropriety, but which it must be admitted do not really shed much light.

"You must have no regrets. These flames will burn on, pure and luminous. Not in some dark brazier with heavy smoke and bitter fragrance, but clear and pure this flame, which never shone for another with such splendor as for you and me, which no other being can conceive. Now I am proud and happy. No more craving, no more desires! No, no: have no regrets!"

And further on: "After the plenitude of your gift of yourself to me, I cannot use words like resignation or despair."

This may be understood as we choose to understand it. We must not forget, however, that the literal sense is not necessarily the true one, for we know that when Mathilde said to him, "I love you," it was his deliverance. This one word was enough, Wagner himself declares, to give to his whole life "a new meaning."

It is, on the other hand, perfectly possible that these words mean exactly what they appear to mean. If Wagner's muse only said no to him after first saying yes, we are confronted by what is certainly a rare instance of flight, coming at the very moment of passion's triumph, serving therefore to maintain passion at the highest point of its burning. This is no mere theory-spinning. If their love was to feed *Tristan* of its substance, it must keep exaltation alive, must never relax until the work was achieved. Not in stirring half-dead ashes could Wagner have written Isolde's death song. What other meaning is there in the letter of 1858 in which he tells Mathilde that from the beginning they had known that their sacrifice was inevitable? "How," he asks, "could the dreadful struggles we have gone through end otherwise than by the vanquishment of all our longings, all our cravings? Did we not realize even in our most burning moments, even when we were nearest to one another, what the end would be?"

This decision was helped by other motives more simply human. For once Wagner appears to have shrunk from the suffering he would cause to others, as Mathilde shrank from those of her husband. Minna, ill and in danger of death, could not have borne the shock, and Wesendonk, his home ruined, would have been left solitary with Mathilde's children. "I made my confession to you," Wagner writes to Mathilde, "and it seemed clear to us that any other alternative would have been a crime the thought of which was unendurable."

This was perfectly sincere, for we must always remember that in his own mind Wagner was then homeless—since the home which had Minna for guardian did not deserve the name, he had none at all! If one studies his reasoning a little, one realizes that, in refusing to fly with Mathilde, Wagner saw himself sacrificing the one home he could have had. The one home! Like the one he had wanted to found with Jenny, or the one which, by smashing Hans von Bulow's life, he was shortly to found with Cosima. For him each such case is a unique case, so that in parting with Mathilde he feels that the world has cast him out and that life has most certainly no further happiness to bestow on him. "With such a wound in my heart, I cannot attempt to build a new home."

For the moment this was true. But Wagner is still far away from the peace towards which he aspires, that same peace longed for so many years earlier by the Dutchman of his Phantom Ship— An intense craving, not for the overflowing delights of passion fulfilled, but for a homeland, for a home. Only a wife, magnificently faithful and devoted, could bring my hero home to this land. Let us consecrate ourselves to that beauteous death in which all these aspirations and longings are embraced and appeased. Let us die happy, with peaceful and shining eyes, with the heavenly smile of the victor. And none shall suffer when we conquer. Farewell my angel, farewell beloved." This beautiful death was to be Isolde's *Unbewüsst, höchste Lust!* And indeed one can see no other possible climax for such a love story. The only way of making it immortal is for the lovers to die before it does.

Let us forget the degrading scenes between Wagner and Minna, between Minna and the Wesendonks, which made the sacrifice necessary. We need only remember that there was also a scene between Wagner and Mathilde, for, although apparently brought about by Minna, it was the deciding factor. Wagner recalls it in his Journal of the 1st of October, 1858: "I felt a terrible pity for you the day you repulsed me—that day you were the victim not of suffering but of passion. You deemed yourself betrayed, you thought all that was noblest in you misunderstood. You seemed to me in that hour like an angel forsaken by God. And precisely as your overwrought condition set me in one act free from my own anguish, it set me to planning how to win you peace and healing."

This rift in a happiness which for Wagner could only mean community of joy in utterly complete sympathy must not be overlooked. For an instant he had seen before him another Mathilde than the one of his dreams; the real woman whom he had made into a Muse stood before him as an angel who had lost her wings. If he was to go on loving her, the time to part had come.

It had come for another reason too—the work was fully formed and only waiting to be born. The music of *Tristan* could not be written with one stormy domestic scene following another; the best thing the Muse could do under the circumstances was to fade out. The artist wants from a woman a love that shall inspire his work, but during the actual composition the thing he asks of her is to leave him alone. It may even be that he must get a little outside his love to put between the lover and the artist the distance which the technical work of creation absolutely demands. The ecstasy of love is no state of soul for a writer. In *L'Economie des Passions*, M. Ch. Lalo quotes a passage from *Massimilia Dont* in which Balzac expresses himself on this subject with copy-book precision: "When an artist has the bad luck to be full of the passion he desires to express, he cannot depict it, for he is the thing itself instead of its mirror. Art comes from the brain and not from the heart. When your subject dominates you, you become its slave and not its master. You are like a king besieged by his subjects. To feel too keenly at the moment of execution means the rebellion of the senses against the mind."

Had Wagner followed this counsel to the letter he would have been what Flaubert called Balzac, "a terrific fellow, not quite first-rate." His art sprang simultaneously and inseparably from brain and heart, but even this great romantic needed a minimum of tranquillity if the brain was to dictate every one of the innumerable notes in the score of *Tristan*.

On August the 17th at five in the morning Wagner left Zurich for Geneva, his heart full of Mathilde and with no pity for Minna. He had no wish to take vengeance on her, but left her to execute her own sentence. "I was going away into solitude," he wrote in his Journal on August the 21st. "There I am at home, there I can love you with all the powers of my soul." For he loves Mathilde more than ever and draws courage from the splendor of their love.

"Yes, we shall indeed forget and overcome all obstacles. One feeling only will be ours, the conviction that a miracle has happened such as nature works only once in centuries and never yet with such noble success." The story of Dante and Beatrice, of Petrarch and Laura is beginning again, but as you see, more splendidly.

He left Geneva on the 25th of August and reached Venice on the 29th. He found it an enchanted city like some far-away world, a world that is dead, in which "there is nothing to give the feel of reality," in which "everything has the objective effect of a work of art." There, in a huge apartment of a palace looking over the Grand Canal, Wagner, in the society of the Erard which he had had sent, was about to cure himself of his own pain and heal Mathilde's wound too. For his pain and hers were one, and both involved in his music. The artist had henceforward one mission: so to live with his art as to console Mathilde by giving her back their love eternally transfigured in the perfection of a masterpiece. At Venice he completed *Tristan*, pure essence of Mathilde and yet his own work—so fully that to keep Mathilde for himself and to keep himself for his work have become one and the same thing: "To keep you for me is to keep myself for my work." The drama of Zurich here attains its climax by receiving its fullness of meaning, for this is the end towards which it was moving from the first:

"So be it, brave Tristan, Lady Isolde. Help me come to my angel's aid. Here you will bleed no more, your wounds will heal and close. Here the world will learn how high and noble is the pain of love at its sublimest, how mournful is desire so agonizing. And you will see me once more—radiant as a god, healed in heart and body, pure—your humble friend."

These words demand to be interpreted quite literally. Wagner has no desire to carry in his heart forever the torment of an unsatisfied passion, and he says precisely what he means when he declares his determination to cure it. The cure will be *Tristan*; for what purpose, indeed, did he endure the anguish, except that he might write the masterpiece? The one is quite precisely the meaning and cause of the other. It was then right, natural, and necessary that the pain of longing should be quieted when he found in his creation the only satisfaction that could be his. The cure meant for Wagner the sealing off, total and permanent, of a part of his life. Looking at his drama when at last it is ended, he sees in it the meaning of the world, and hence also he sees Mathilde who revealed it to him. But this Mathilde is triumphant, untouchable henceforth by the sorrow which she had to suffer with him only that his art might set them both free. "*Tristan* will still cost me much effort, but I feel that when it is finished a marvellous epoch in my life will have found its completion. Henceforward I shall look out upon the world with a spirit renewed, with calm, deep, and clear insight, and beyond the world I shall be gazing at you."

This is all very well, but the lines leave one wondering whether art was not the real reason underlying the sacrifice apparently offered to the demands of morality. The duet of the second act of *Tristan* is too beautiful for the most passionate lovers to be able to sustain it for a whole lifetime. When the third act of this frenzied drama is ended one feels they must die of exhaustion. What could be done about it? Wagner needed Mathilde only to write *Tristan*, after which she would be useless. But she would have become useless far earlier had their affair ended in the common-places of divorce and remarriage instead of culminating in the tragic renunciation of which death was the only possible symbol.

Thus the completion of *Tristan* at Venice did indeed bring to an end for Wagner "a marvellous epoch" in his life, for the death dealt to the two lovers by his art makes sacred the end of his passion for Mathilde and hers for him. Their love reaches at the same time its end and its goal. The ear alone would discover it as we listen to Isolde singing that "song of death" which is the crowning point of the drama: a song vibrating with trembling joy, ecstatic, almost unbearable. And reading the words one recognizes it for what it is, Wagner's most beautiful hymn to his own music. What is this wonderful and sensitive song springing from Tristan's dead body, and why does Isolde invite us to listen if she alone could hear it? How well we know that delight that overflows in tears, that phrase which harmonizes all things by uttering them totally, which reaches to our depths, which draws us upwards and enfolds us so that we are totally immersed in its immense resonance.

One would not dare translate such poetry unless the divine music could be heard with it, for, as Wagner tells us, the poetry is born of the music. But at least we must ask with Isolde, "Do not you feel it, friends? Do not you see it?" This hymn answering the song that springs from Tristan's body is offered by Mathilde to her *Tristan* through Wagner. The artist is officiating with joy at the completion of a masterpiece, the birth of which is the death of their love.

This had been foreseen by both. "A year ago," Wagner writes in his Journal of the 18th of September, 1858, "I finished the poem of *Tristan* and I brought the last act to you. You came with me to the chair in front of the sofa, you embraced me and said, 'Now I have nothing more to wish for.'" Nothing indeed, for in this poem she had all she really expected from their love. But how clearly he, on the other hand, saw that his art ruled his life. "My child," he writes in the Journal of the 3rd of October, "the sublime Buddha was right in banishing art so rigorously. Who can realize better than I that it is this miserable art that eternally flings me back into the sorrows of life, into the contradictions of existence." Certainly he meant Mathilde, for if Wagner could have given up his art he could give her up too, forget her and be happy. But how could he create *Tristan* unless he gazed constantly upon her?—which is exactly what he did. He cries out, "Help me, stay beside me"—and the more he beseeches her, the further she departs, for every time that she answers his call a voice is heard saying, "In this world where you accept this suffering that your work may be achieved she will never belong to you." He could only write *Tristan* with his heart full of Mathilde; he must think of her, he must remember that she was lost forever: "What matter if only *Tristan* be happily concluded?"

Peace gradually came to him as the work went forward. Why should the poet claim his Muse, since she is already wholly his? "I feel a divine satisfaction. My passion is dead because it is utterly appeased." Let Mathilde bring up her children, let her be happy, he will not be jealous. They will see each other again no doubt, but in a dream, for they will be themselves and yet not themselves. Like Petrarch with Laura, Wagner dreams of an old age when he can dare to go back to Mathilde, "when all suffering and all bitterness have been overcome." Perhaps one morning she will even come in through the study with its green hangings and receive his soul into a farewell embrace. Wagner is dreaming...but not for long: he awakes with the sudden splendor of this terrific phrase, "Now back to *Tristan* that, through his mediation, the deep art of a resounding silence may speak to you in my name."

In these words he tells her all he wants to say, all that *Tristan* itself has told us since. Because life has separated them the two lovers are henceforth inseparable. "As to us two, you and me, near or far, we are united, we are one sole being."

It would be endless to follow the winding path of this slow cure, delayed sometimes by Mathilde's imprudence, for she followed Wagner's lead in this matter, but haltingly and at a distance, having herself no art in which to seek salvation. She was suffering and she sent Wagner the journal in which she said so. Wagner thereupon talked (on October the 30th) of rejoining her—but he stayed on in Venice out of consideration for Mathilde's children. On the 1st of November, All Saints Day, he thought of flinging himself into the Grand Canal, and even went so far as "to grasp the balcony to hoist himself over it"—but he did not jump—still out of consideration for Mathilde and her children. She urged him to find comfort in his art, but he made the admirable reply that art "is for me neither consolation nor compensation, it is only the accompaniment of my profound harmony with you." Everything in him breaks up if he notes the least discord between their two souls. "With you I can do all things, without you nothing. Nothing.... Believe me, my only love. You hold me in the hollow of your hand: with you alone I can reach the crowning achievement."

He is in fact reaching it, for *Tristan* is now at the second act. "What music it is becoming! The rest of my life I shall be able to work only at this music I have never done anything like it before: I am living wholly in this music, I don't want to know, I would rather not know, when it will be finished. I live in it eternally. And with me...." And with me? You.

Wagner went on writing his drama, patiently, lovingly, as he had never written before. "I am working," he wrote to Eliza Wille, "as though I never want to be busy about anything else for the rest of my life. And *Tristan* is thereby becoming more beautiful than all my earlier work put together. The least little phrase has the importance of an entire act, I am taking so much pains over it." On the 10th of March, 1859, the second act was completed: the problem, thought insoluble by many, he has solved "as no problem has ever been solved before. Up to now it is the apex of my art."

And how much of himself he has poured into it. The fire, he wrote to Mathilde on April the 10th, "was burning, was almost consuming me." While as to the third act, "this *Tristan*, this child of mine, is becoming something terrific. Oh this final act!!! I am afraid the opera will be prohibited—unless a bad performance turns it into a parody: only mediocre performances can save me. First-rate ones would drive the audience mad—I cannot doubt it. I was certain to run into this trouble again, unhappy man that I am."

Yet we might well say also "happy man." While he is giving himself calmly to a restful working out of the instrumentation, Kant, Schiller, and Buddha are mingling their lessons in his mind with those of his own experience. He perceives with Kant that space, time, causation—in short, the whole structure of the universe—are the product of our thought. He tells himself that the artist's function is precisely to anticipate experience, and that, in Schiller's words, what the poet knows is *true* because it has never been. But Wagner goes on to ask whether the miraculous effect of genius is not actually that what never has *been* ends by *being*, and takes flesh in a masterpiece, and finds existence in that very experience which the idea anticipated. What matter, then, if the idea takes flesh in the life of the poet also, because the experience will finally be purified by the art in the light of which it exists. Its aesthetic interest would lose nothing by becoming also morally interesting. Thus *Tristan* is burning up all that is human in this love affair: "You feel it all, you know it! Yes, you, and perhaps no

one else." Never did poet associate his muse more closely with his
art, and Wagner pays her the highest compliment at the moment
when he is demanding from her the most grievous renunciation.
But he is demanding nothing less from himself, for it is over himself that Wagner is weeping as he writes with tear-filled eyes the
exulting music which accompanies Kurwenal's words to Tristan:
"Now you are at home, at home in your land, your own land, the
land of your fathers, in your own fields, under your remembered
sky. Here you will be healed of your wounds." The tragedy of it
is unheard-of, Wagner declares, it is utterly crushing, and all the
more so because Tristan himself remains indifferent, for him it is
so much noise. But the noise is full of meaning for the poet: the
death of Tristan is to be in truth the cure of his own wounds, his
own resurrection.

The redemption wrought by the work seems to have preceded its completion. Wagner returned to Switzerland near the
Wesendonks, and his long letter to Mathilde on the 30th of May,
1859, shows him already full of Parsifal. One masterpiece drives
out another, and *Tristan* was completed in Lucerne towards the
end of July. Wagner now saw Mathilde again quite freely, and it
would be hard to tell which held most truth of the two formulas:
"he still loved her" or "he loved her no longer."

He still loved Mathilde, but no longer the same Mathilde,
and not with the same love. "There is no longer any illusion for
me to make use of," he was to say in 1861. As a useful illusion
Mathilde was dead, and the more he saw of her in her home,
surrounded by her husband and children, the better he understood that the woman he had loved—whom he loved still as she
was when he used to love her—had her supreme existence within
himself. Wagner was speaking the exact truth when he called her
"my child," for she is indeed the work of his genius, the daughter
of his creative imagination.

89

On this point nothing can take the place of the incomparable letter written at Lucerne, on the 4th of April, 1859, and inserted by Wagner in his Journal the day after his return from Venice, well before the completion of *Tristan*, when he had just seen Mathilde for the first time since their separation:

"The dream of seeing each other again has been realized! Yes, we have met once more. But was it not still a dream? What difference was there between what I experienced during those hours spent in your house and that other heavenly dream of my return which had been haunting me? I might almost say that this melancholy, serious dream which my memory can hardly recall is more real to me than the actual meeting. I do not think I saw you clearly, thick mists separated us through which we scarcely heard the sound of each other's voice. You also, I fancy, did not see me, a ghost entered your house in my place. Did you recognize me? Oh, heavens, I begin to realize it: this is the road towards sanctity! Life itself, the reality of things, take on more and more the shape of a dream; the senses are deadened, with eyes wide open I see nothing, my ears are keenly attentive but no longer hear the voice that speaks. We do not see the place where we are. Our eyes are fixed on distance. The present has no existence, the future is nothingness.—Does my work indeed merit that I should give it my entire being? What about you, what about your children— life must go on."

I hope it will not seem too startling if I say, with full awareness of the difference in the events, the inflections and the very different levels, that this return of 1859, while not at all its equivalent, is comparable with the morrow of the Baudelaire-Sabatier love affair. In both cases the poet was confronted with the woman, and in neither case did he recognize her. It was not when he was gazing upon Madame Wesendonk that Wagner saw the true Mathilde but when he was gazing at Isolde. Nor is it where Wagner is present that Madame Wesendonk recognizes him, it is where Tristan is that she sees Wagner. The work of art which has risen out of life lowers, so to speak, its mantle over life, covers it, drowns it, in a radiant mist which becomes for the artist the actual reality. And not for the artist only but for us also, when for four hours the music of *Tristan* has carried us away into a dream world out of which we come staggering, vague and lost, astonished by that so-called real world of the streets whose continued existence is felt like a hurt. Try to imagine, then, what the years spent in creating it must have meant for the creator himself of this poetic universe. For Wagner, for Mathilde, so well aware of the greatness of the work with which the imperious genius of the poet had associated her, everything went on as though they belonged no longer to this world but to another, better, purer, wholly justified by its very perfection, to which they could only gain access by renouncing this one. This language reminds us irresistibly of another to which the masters of a spirituality not only purer but of a different order have long familiarized us. And it comes back to us later when we read again the strange phrase in which this man, devoured by human passions, declared to Mathilde Wesendonk that he sometimes felt himself on the verge of sanctity.

V. A Philosophic Muse

Man can have a muse for anything he creates, even for philosophy. It must be admitted, however, that truth once again confounded probability when it chose Positivism to put under the patronage of an Inspiration. The story of Clotilde de Vaux is so extraordinary that it has been told many times.[1] It is essential to recall it here, for it casts much light on the persistence of the general plan determining affairs of this kind. It must be told not for its own sake, but as the story of a Muse, underlining the features that show its relationship with all the rest. And even the founder of Positivism may have something to tell us of poetry and music.

In 1842 Comte had finished his *Cours de philosophie positive*, and we need only look at the outside of the six volumes to appreciate the immensity of the intellectual effort that they cost him. But Comte, having been Aristotle, now wanted to be St. Paul. Reverting almost immediately to a series of reflections the origin of which went back beyond his Positive philosophy, he undertook the elaboration of his political Positivism, but the writing was interrupted when he had hardly begun it. For Comte underwent a nervous crisis which he himself described in his letter of the 27th of June, 1845, to John Stuart Mill, as consisting of incurable sleeplessness, "together with a gentle but persistent melancholy, great difficulty in breathing, for a long time accompanied by extreme weakness." He promised his English correspondent further "interesting details" which may in fact be found nearly a year later, in the letter of the 6th of May, 1846, which is important in relation to the subject of this book.

When he wrote, the affair was already at an end. "On the 5th of April (1846) I witnessed the death at the beginning of her 32nd year of the wonderful friend to whom last year I dedicated my philosophical letter on the Social Commemoration (of which I sent you a copy in July). Now that this is a secret belonging, alas, to myself alone (because no review was willing to publish it) I can make known to a heart as gifted as yours to understand me, that it was a question of my first and my last love. Our mutual love always remained as pure as it was deep. In my unfortunate marriage there was nothing but exaggerated generosity, which was my response to what I took to be total trust. At bottom, though my heart always craved for sympathy, it had remained exceptionally virgin down to my first intercourse with this magnificent woman; our organic harmony was strengthened by a sad similarity in our moral situation, although her domestic unhappiness was far greater, and certainly more undeserved, than mine."

His greatest admirers could not persuade one that Comte wrote well. Apart from a few phrases admirably coined and quite unforgettable, which after all is something, he fumbles, hesitates

---

1. Never better than by H. Gouhier in his thrilling *Life of Auguste Comte* (Paris: Gallimard, 1931).

over his words, and ends often enough by missing the right one. To that must be added a pompous use of platitudes which would provoke a smile if we were dealing with a lesser man. But he does make himself understood; he is lavish in precise details about intimate matters on which precision is usually only too rare. Married, unhappily married, separated from his wife, he had still kept his heart inviolate and began at the age of forty-eight to experience his first and last love with a young woman who was only thirty-two the day she died. For both of them love was, very properly, as pure as it was deep. All the same the philosopher admits that, over and above the moral similarity in their situation, he felt what he oddly christens an organic harmony with this magnificent woman. As with Petrarch in the past but contrary to Baudelaire about ten years later, experience did not with the philosopher come forward to confirm this mutual belief in their "organic harmony." But the strange destiny governing these stories appears to know that the spiritual fruitfulness of their affection demands physical frustration.

According to rule, also, Comte's passionate love broke out at the exact moment when it was needed for his work. "The deciding attack of this virtuous passion coincided last year with the initial working out of my second great work." The crisis of which he spoke in 1845 to Stuart Mill was by then more complicated and, in one sense, deeper than simple nervous depression. Comte was suffering from the great anguish of a genius in childbirth, and was ready for that midwifery in reverse where the woman delivers the man from the burden he is carrying, so that overwhelmed with gratitude he often imagines that it was she who had conceived it. So it was with our philosopher, now that he had in one act lost both his happiness and the beloved friend who was to superintend the completion of his work. "I felt with delight the admirable spontaneous harmony of this private love with my public mission, at the moment when I was beginning a new career in philosophy in which the heart would have at least as great a natural share as the mind itself."

It may be noted, however, that Comte does not give Clotilde the credit of any philosophical discovery. He speaks of a spontaneous harmony between this love and his own mission. He does not say, even in 1846, that Clotilde had revealed to him the philosophic importance of the heart, but only that she had caused him to undergo although late, a deep initiation of the affections, the last and indispensable completion of my entire preparation for philosophy: "without it I could not adequately have fulfilled my final mission of fundamental service for the mighty regeneration of humanity." Awkwardly as he expresses himself, what Comte is saying is true with a truth greater than that of his own love affair: the Muse affects the work only through the man who creates it.

We must glance at the story of those two years. In 1844, visiting a former student of the Polytechnic who thought of him to some degree as his Master, August Comte met his young disciple's sister. The husband of this Madame Clotilde de Vaux, a teacher at Meru, had run away in 1839 leaving an empty cash box behind him. He was never seen again. After less than four years of marriage this delightful young woman of twenty-four found herself alone, entirely destitute, not even a widow, but in the eyes of the law the legitimate wife of a swindler on the run. This was the history that she herself told as a romance in a story called *Lucie* which Armand Marrast's *National* published in two installments on June the 20th and 21st, 1845. She paints a beautiful picture of herself, and with some justification. It was true that the guilty husband had abandoned "after some months of marriage a young woman possessed of great beauty and the highest qualities." There is about Clotilde a touch of Corneille's "point of honor" and of the moral heroics of the Grand Siècle, when she describes Lucie, that is to say herself, as "one of those noble women who can more easily accept disaster than act shamefully." And again, "it is unworthy of a great soul to spread abroad the anguish that it feels."

Madame de LaFayette would doubtless have approved of such maxims but by no means of the fundamental thesis of the story. For Clotilde de Vaux's *Lucie* is a vehement protest against the social injustice of which she was the victim, and we may be certain that August Comte gave much thought to the arguments in her appeal. Lucie-Clotilde cannot remarry. The law forbids her. She might possibly put up with that, if renouncing marriage did not at the same time mean renouncing the joys of family life. "Oh, my dear friend, the thought of motherhood haunts my heart with a youthful and ardent longing." We shall see what Comte thought up later as an answer to the problem which Lucie struggled with and found insoluble, to attain motherhood and remain a virgin. Comte presents a fascinating variation of the species Wagner, who found himself so often, at the moment of writing a lyric drama, in a personal position similar to that of the heroes in his poem. In this story everything happened as though the Muse-to-be had sketched in advance the scenario of the drama which the philosopher was going to live. For Lucie was loved by Maurice, who asked himself, "To what end does society leave a man a wife when the only children he can have are bastards?" By what right does it impose loneliness and celibacy upon one of its members? Maurice's mother, a worthy spokesman of social prejudice, would allow her son to think as an atheist but not to give up the sacraments. Moreover, the law forbids this marriage. A petition from Maurice to the Chambre des Deputés, asking that divorce should be allowed at any rate when a husband has betrayed his wife, encounters violent and widespread opposition. Lucie's heart is broken. She offers Maurice his freedom and advises him to found a family. But she herself dies of the affair and he kills himself beside her dead body before the doctor can forestall his dread design. There remains nothing for the doctor but to preach the heroine's funeral sermon.

"Those who knew the remarkable and unfortunate woman whose loss I am lamenting will understand the fatal passion which she inspired. Hers was one of those rare organisms in which heart and spirit have each their full share. No woman knew better than she the splendor of her office: she would have been a perfect wife and mother. Alas, as I saw her expiring in my arms at the age most proper for living, I realized with grief how little power man has to undo the evil that he creates." Not one of these words was lost for Comte, especially as, when he read them for the first time, Lucie was still alive and Maurice's place not filled. As to the laws, he was of a stature to get them altered.

Clotilde then was an author before she became a Muse. But unlike another to be examined presently, she claimed no rights over the work of the man whom she inspired. She was even a poet, for besides *Lucie* and an unfinished story called *Wilhelmine* she has left us *Les Pensées d'une Fleur*: verses which are not much more feeble—and that is quite feeble enough—than some of Chateaubriand's. However, it was not these works which chiefly interested the philosopher; it was the young and beautiful woman whom he met at his disciple's house at a time when his heart was "exceptionally virgin," and all his defences down.

Comte knew himself too well to have any illusions in this matter, but he was now too old to pursue the amorous adventures of his youth—one of which had ended up in his unhappy marriage with the girl, Caroline Massin. The story of this need not be told, for Comte's friends themselves do not agree about it and it would teach us nothing on the subject that interests us. The one point to be noticed is that Comte, as candidate for the role of Maurice (suicide apart), was also in the position of Lucie. Married, and unhappily married, Comte felt about his wife what Clotilde felt about her husband, and he too had to bear the slavery of a separation that yet held him with an unbreakable chain. She was still the wife of Monsieur de Vaux. He was still the husband of Caroline Massin. Like her he was without home or children, like her he was exiled from family joys. In short, when he compared the position of Clotilde de Vaux with his own he saw in her the victim, "more unhappy than he and more spotless, of a similar calamity, so that her moral liberty of action was even more strongly founded than his." Overwhelmed by exactly similar misfortune, were they not morally free to unite their tragedies and to console one another?

Of all the stories of this type there is none better known to us, and the hundred and eighty-three letters which make up their correspondence would really be an *embarras de richesses* were it not that everything worked out in closest conformity with the traditional pattern. Comte's first letter, for naturally he is the first one to write, is dated April the 30th, 1845, at midday. He offers Clotilde a translation of Fielding's *Tom Jones* of which he himself possesses the original. The usual thanks follow and the usual courtesies, a visit from Clotilde to Comte, visits from Comte to Clotilde at the home of her parents. Nothing could be more normal. Clotilde, as we have said, was extremely intelligent, lonely, unhappy, and even despairing. It can be imagined that the society of such a man as Comte was a very pleasant distraction for her, all the more because his age, his appearance, his rank as a master of ideas and his solemn language in no way announced a probable lover. It is clear that she did not understand him, but his letter of the 17th of May, 1845, should have been warning enough, for the philosopher was already speaking of the "sweet unity of feeling" which had gradually drawn him towards her.

She had made a mistake, and her mistake helps us to understand the psychology of certain Muses. Clotilde would never have the slightest physical love for Comte, but she did love him all the same, sincerely and perhaps deeply. The brotherhood of mind and heart which he had offered at first, and with which he had to be satisfied at last, was for her a precious and unhoped-for boon, the only comfort she could still receive from man, this woman who hoped for none from the God in whom she did not believe. Their wholly spiritual intercourse could be something very beautiful, and in one sense it was: but the young woman soon saw simply one more misfortune added to all that already overwhelmed her when Comte, having awakened in her heart the mirage of this oasis, startlingly unleashed a wild beast which began to lay it waste.

That the philosopher should promise to dedicate to her his *Système de politique positive* was pleasing enough. When he declared that "by restoring to life the play of his sweetest private feelings" she would effectually assist his philosophic impetus, this too was quite acceptable. It all meant the offer of a role as Muse of Positivism which nothing forbade her to play. But when Comte talked of "these precious feelings, these intimate outpourings, these delicious tears" which brought him "enrapturing vigils" and even made him ill, Clotilde understood very well what he was really telling her. I shall soon be coming to see you again "at your parents' home (I almost said our parents)," he wrote. He was certainly a fast worker. As he said in his note of May the 20th, this had been a "decisive letter." Thereupon Clotilde put Comte in his place—which he accepted and in which he promised to remain.

Let us hear what Clotilde had to say. Her answer of May the 21st is well worth reading and strikes once for all the note which she maintained up to the end. "I have suffered too much,

Monsieur, not to speak sincerely, and if I did not answer your letter of Saturday it was because of the painful feelings it awakened in me which I could not have managed to hide from you. When I accepted your friendship and the interest you took in me I hoped, I own, that it would add to my happiness and your own. It has made me unhappy to be forced to fear the opposite. If I had not long formed the habit of hiding my feelings I should, I am sure, have inspired more pity in you than tenderness. For the last year I have asked myself each night whether I had the strength to live through the next day… It is not from such a state of mind that rash acts come… Spare me these emotions as I would like to spare you: I feel no less keenly than you do. Goodbye, Monsieur Comte. Believe, please, that you have my true affection and esteem. These I offer you forever."

Clotilde is in the great tradition of letter-writing women who know that everything can be said if you never raise your voice. But she was miles away from suspecting what was really happening. She begs Comte to spare her if he loves her—but he does not love her for herself but for himself. He needs her for his own "moral development," for his "moral resurrection," and he needs all this to help in the "new-born elaboration" of his "second great work, which, far from suffering from such assistance, will certainly be all the better for it," as a pleasant experience has already directly proved to him.

It is hard to believe our eyes: Comte needs Clotilde to write the *Système de politique positive* as Wagner needed Mathilde to write *Tristan*. It does not seem at all the same thing, for *Tristan* is a direct translation of the love that Wagner felt for his Muse, whereas the *Système* extols something quite different from Comte's passion for his. And yet this is not entirely the case, for whether she desires it or not, Clotilde is to be seized upon by the *Système*. She is to get inside it, to work upon it, to modify it from within. The non-conformist Positivists later put the responsibility of what they considered deviations in the Master's thought upon this love of Comte's, and Comte never defended himself by saying that Clotilde had no part in the evolution of his doctrine. On the contrary, those who refused to believe that she did affect it were excommunicated. To maintain in Comte's presence that the *Système de politique positive* owed nothing to Clotilde would have been no less rash than to congratulate Wagner on having written *Tristan* without Mathilde Wesendonk.

For the moment everything settled down and life was organized on the basis of the treaty they had agreed upon. Comte continued to see Clotilde in her home. They played music together, a thing which is always risky but which indicates how high a value Clotilde attached to this friendship. As for the philosopher, he resigned himself, but unwillingly. He admits that affection in him is not as "virtuous" as of course it is in Clotilde, but he trusts that it may become so. Meanwhile he writes to her on May the 24th: "The indispensable transformation that you are obliged to prescribe in my feelings is much more painful than you can imagine." On the 28th of May Comte in his inimitable style adds the information that the first crisis is happily ended. "The coarseness of my sex doubtless forced upon me this transitional tempest before I could reach that pure state of true friendship which feminine delicacy allowed you to reach instantly with no such preamble." We are inclined to smile at that, but when, a little further on, Comte reminds Clotilde that, as he never knew what passion was before, he has a claim that the thoughtlessness of his youth should be excused, we feel quite disarmed.

No more embarrassing conversations then. Comte will not bring distress into a sensitive heart. "Let us talk only from the head and let us try to introduce as much gaiety as possible." This seemed an admirable program. The Feast of St. Clotilde was celebrated by a philosophical letter on the *Commémoration sociale*, but something must have happened after June the 2nd, or it may merely have been, as Comte's reply suggests, that Clotilde again became aware of danger. For on June the 5th she wrote to him that, having loved for the last two years a man who loved her but whom she could not marry, she had been obliged to get away from him if she were to keep the strength to live. Her heart is broken. Let Comte give up all hope and stop coming to see her; as "a hopeless love kills soul and body alike," let him struggle to overcome his own unfortunate affection.

Comte, thus dismissed, expressed his surprise at its being done in this fashion, and after a delay of fifteen days. He apologized for having believed that Clotilde was heart-whole, although resolute to remain so. In short he had a rival of whom no one had told him. The affair was definitely at an end. They would say no more about it and he would come to her house no more (unless she invited him); but every time he was free, Wednesday or Friday, he would spend the evening with Clotilde's worthy family, with which Comte would in every way find delight in being "fused." He will now become her spiritual father, the same relation which he already has with her brother. Henceforth he will call her Clotilde, and since there is no other way for him to bring happiness to her he will begin to work at her "improvement." Then come some observations on the art of writing in which Comte shows himself shrewd enough to perceive that the style of Clotilde's letters is better than that of her novels.

When Clotilde published *Lucie* Comte read and re-read it with enthusiasm. Of course he realized that she was Lucie, why could not he be Maurice? Whereupon his imagination once more got to work. "Oh," he wrote, on the 3rd of July, "if ever I am free again I am fully determined to have no other wife but you." He will remain unmarried if Clotilde will not have him—so it was not, then, marriage which he had first offered her! Clotilde repeated her refusal; even the position of an "honorable wife" did not tempt her. Confidence in his devotion, esteem, attachment, everything of that kind that Comte desires, but nothing more. "I will be your friend if you wish, but never anything else." And Clotilde concludes, "a false or ambiguous situation is impossible for me, and I have tried my best to make my position clear to you." Between the young woman and the philosopher, it is pretty clear where the good sense and definite ideas are to be found.

And yet she went on seeing him and even visiting him "as a friend" once a week, whenever she could manage it. No doubt she realized that this big child needed her, nor was she ignorant of the fact that he was a great man—and she herself being a literary lady...all this she says with bourgeois elegance when promising him a visit. "We have made our pact and you will find that you lose nothing through my companionship since you really desire it. I have always loved the society of distinguished men from whom there is so much to gain." Where Clotilde deluded herself was when she declared that she had never been afraid of any man, because "a woman always inspires the sort of feeling that she desires." Not so when an Auguste Comte was involved, and this she was to discover before very long.

For the moment she was the philosopher's disciple, or at least obedient to his advice. Marrast offered to publish her in the *Nationale.* She accepted his offer and proposed to discuss problems of education, but Comte showed her that this would be a tremendous mistake. Clotilde, it seems, quickly lost interest in this kind of collaboration. The real events were all occurring inside Comte's mind, for, once assured of definite rejection by his Muse, he began to turn her into a divinity. In an immense letter of August the 5th, 1845, the philosopher explains to Clotilde that, thanks to her, his personal affections will tend directly to the perfecting of his social action. Like Wagner, he found himself by a miracle in the situation called for to complete his work. He ended an interminable discourse by saying to his Muse, "I trust that after these explanations you can be in no real doubt about the happy philosophic results which I expect from our eternal friendship." She has already become "St. Clotilde," and it is in a pious attitude of mind that he undertakes his second great work. His more practical Muse borrows fifty francs from him on the 11th of August, 1845. Comte is enchanted, offers her more and, far from being discouraged, raises an "altar" to Clotilde in front of which he invokes her as a refreshment from his work and feels the birth of his highest inspirations.

The "cult" of Clotilde was born; not just a simple sentimental veneration, but a concrete worship of which Comte was to remain the priest up to the end of his life. The new saint having been so imprudent as to seal her spiritual union with the philosopher by a "holy kiss," granted in the presence of her parents, he became as wildly excited as a troubadour to whom the same gift had been granted by his lady. And not without reason, as it turned out: for Clotilde's imagination was also at work, and on September the 5th, 1845, she wrote to her spiritual father. She was touched by his goodness, she had given the matter much thought, her dreams were of motherhood, and if he believed he could accept the full responsibilities of family life, he could tell her so and she would make her decision.

This letter Comte read and then re-read on his knees in front of the altar of Clotilde. Naturally enough, the volcano erupted. "Since yesterday I look upon you as my one true wife, not only wife to be but wife now and forever." He did not lose his head, however, for so many legal, social, and other difficulties stood between them and their union that if marriage was in question all was uncertain. Comte indicated this in his reply: "Your generous confidence will permit this union to receive *if necessary* its final pledge." In short, "with delight but without impetuosity" he would accept the risks of fatherhood in an illegal union. It must, of course, be kept secret and had better be entered upon without formalities. In any case the decision rested with Clotilde, the matter of fulfillment following the consent she has just yielded (sic) "will always be laid in her hands with respectful deference."

Clotilde asked for a few months' delay and Comte agreed to this, but not without askng for an immediate "pledge of the alliance," a "definite guarantee of the indissolubility of their union"—in short, for a concrete "concession" with all the risk it might bring. After all, if maternity did result, it would only be what Clotilde had always asked for. Alas, this respectful demand faced Madame de Vaux with something far too definite and real. To have a child, you must accept a father; she began to beat a retreat. She hoped Comte would forgive her rash remarks. She still felt herself "helpless" to give him anything beyond the limits of affection. "I am incapable of giving myself without love. I felt it yesterday. I, too, am ill. Do not presume on the power which I meant to give you."

Without love! These words were clear enough. But notice with what amazing dialectic the philosopher in his letter of September the 8th justifies the "modest installment" of which he asks her to make the "concession." One point in his answer is of interest to us, and it is the point which Clotilde did not understand. It was no vulgar personal pleasure that he hoped for from this "sacred pledge," but a guarantee of their complete union and the impetus which "the habitual feeling of internal satisfaction" would give to his spirit. It was unfortunate for him that Clotilde should feel such revolt against the kind of collaboration with the *Système de politique positive* offered her by her philosopher. The young woman replied quite definitely that she had had enough of it all, that Comte was wearying her, and that if he went on, there would be real exasperation. "I know marriage and I know myself better than the most learned man in the world. Do not attempt the least discussion of my feelings." A word to the wise.

From now on the business dragged along in a melancholy fashion, coming to no issue. Tormented by the unconscious egoism of genius, the sensitive Clotilde dreaded "the evil of an irregular affair, however legitimate and honorable were the reasons for it."

Never did a Muse speak so well the language of common sense, and it is irresistibly comic that she should have been its mouthpiece to a philosopher so fanatically set upon a definitive foundation for morality. Clotilde in fact was unhappily languishing towards her end, but the more he realized that he was losing her, the more Comte turned her into an ideal. Not that he wholly loosened his grasp: letters continued. There was advice from him on the shaping of Clotilde's new novel, there was kindness from Clotilde, who carried her trust in him to the point of borrowing a further hundred francs. This "communism" delighted Comte and did not in the least lessen either her power as an Inspiration or the "private adoration" of her from which he drew the "daily thrill" needed for his work and which he could not get from "the inadequate food furnished by his universal love of Humanity." She was for him Humanity in the concrete, and it was in her that he loved Humanity concretely.

There were, of course, minor crises, for every time Clotilde offered him her "heart," Comte hoped anew for the rest of her. Meanwhile his soul underwent "the profound transformation of a chrysalis" through Clotilde he entered upon a "fresh existence," purer and deeper than the one out of which she had drawn him. After all (he told her) the love of d'Alembert for Mlle. de Lespinasse was worth more than Rousseau's, that most eloquent of sophists, for Madame d'Hondetot. No doubt Comte was right, but after all poor Rousseau sighed in vain for the favors of Madame d'Hondetot, whereas d'Alembert's love for Mademoiselle de Lespinasse—had the most normal conclusion—and after d'Alembert came the Comte de Guibert... All this did not worry Comte. Clotilde wrote him that she had taken a purgative; he replied that every morning in front of her altar he recited his loving prayer to Saint Clotilde and re-read extracts from her letters, "those most suitable to mark out the steps in their holy love." Nothing discouraged him, nor for that matter her either. Henceforward they were to go forward "leaning upon each other," exchanging from time to time the affectionate kiss of friends, hardly knowing which gave or which received it, in a pitiable confusion of love, jealousy, music, Positivism, money, and cod liver oil—until the final catastrophe, when Clotilde, after a last attempt to offer him more than her friendship, died in Comte's arms. They were alone, for he had shut the door of her room in the face of her bewildered parents.

No judgment is possible of such a story. Like all who love, Comte and Clotilde brought each other suffering. Unable to give herself totally, she had hoped to keep forever an affection that did so much for her, to get him to "forget their difference of sex"; but apart from the final letters which are dominated by her illness Comte did not leave her ignorant that for him this was impossible. Moreover, his prayer to Clotilde reminded him every morning: "a true friend in the world of the present, and in the near future an honored spouse."

Let us accept with Comte himself the good and the bad together. It was true, as Clotilde once told him, that Comte had the heart of a knight and that it was great good fortune for an unhappy woman to have met such a friend. Already dying, she accepted his help, and with the supreme delicacy of a woman she strove to make herself into his disciple. But she was much more to him than an assistant, becoming both a light and a guide. Aware of the originality and logical continuity of his own thought, Comte was able to tell Clotilde before she died the exact nature and limits of his debt to her. "This is the supreme service for which my total effort will always be indebted, my beloved Clotilde, to your adorable influence. You have greatly contributed towards making the second half of my philosophical career superior to the first: if not in regard to the purity and originality of my ideas, at least in the fullness and vigor of their final systematization."

It was under this young woman's influence that—instead of peacefully building up towards the conclusion contained in its premises—the heavy edifice of Positivism rocked violently on its foundations. By affirming once and for all the primacy of the heart, this philosophy turned resolutely in the direction of religion.

Beatrice is dead, Laura is dead, Clotilde is dead, and for her, as for her predecessors, the hour of transfiguration has arrived. There is nothing arbitrary in bringing these names together, for while he had read and admired Petrarch—a conspicuous figure in his Library of Positivism—Comte was a fervent devotee of Dante. In his *Système de politique positive* he informs us that for the last seven years he had read a canto daily, and we can see that he made use of the original, since his quotations are in Italian. The great figure of the *altissimo poeta* haunted him, and it would be endless to relate the parts played in his imagination by the man of whom he once wrote: "the two intellectuals typical of the modern world, Dante and Descartes." The *Divina Commedia* was for him a "sacred book," whose teaching was inexhaustible. But what should especially rivet our attention is his crowning decision to add to those two shining historical couples, Dante and

Beatrice, Petrarch and Laura, a third who should far transcend them: Comte and Clotilde.

Positivism, he felt, could do better in this matter than the Middle Ages, for however high chivalry had raised Woman, it could only rank her second—God came first. She was, Comte declared, "crushed beneath the beliefs of theology" from which he had now set humanity free. Henceforth "man would bow the knee no longer except before woman." The "doctrine" he was introducing "would of necessity establish the adoration of women," an ideal which even the splendid chivalry of the Middle Ages did not dare to conceive. Chivalry was at one and the same time splendid and out of date, just as in politics the Conservatives were at once noble and reactionary. Comte's thought is regulated with striking consistency by a rhythm in two movements—he crowns his predecessors before sacrificing them. Nor is this unreasonable, for next to being Comte himself nothing could be greater than to have been his precursor.

It was only just that Clotilde should enter into glory with him and that the Humanity of the future should hold them in a close unity. Comte has forgotten henceforward that if he had had his way, Clotilde would have been his mistress. All that is wiped out, obliterated, expunged from history, to give place to a chaste and pure love which is all that the High Priest of Humanity has any recollection of having felt for his companion in immortality. Lifted above social and religious prejudices, above legal formalities, she was his wife. Madame Comte is still alive, but he is a widower, widowed of Clotilde, in widowhood which his desires proclaim eternal, so that their marriage too may become eternal. We had better not get lost in the labyrinth of doctrinal justifications through which Comte gives himself the right to think whatever he wants to think. Like Rousseau he is a past master in the art. The historical examples he cites make clear to us anyhow what he wants to convince us of, that even although the monogamy of the West is one of the most valuable institutions we owe to the Middle Ages and must at all cost be upheld, yet a man may not in fact be the husband of the woman he married. He may have as his true spouse a woman of whom he is not the husband. The Middle Ages, dominated by theological absolutism, could allow no exceptions to a rule once it was established, but what is the great discovery of Positivism except that "all is relative"? The philosophy of Positivism alone can "reconcile the unavoidably general quality of rules of varying morality with the justifiable exceptions called for in all practical regulations." It need hardly be added that the spiritual marriage of Clotilde and Comte is the most richly justified of all these exceptions. It literally confirms the rule.

The whole thing is a perfect example of reasoning in a circle. First come the historical precedents which justify, in the name of true monogamy, that a man should be the eternal widower of a woman who was never his wife. There have been cases in which public opinion rightly "buried in the same coffin hearts which death could not divide." Why should not posterity unite in this fashion the hearts of Clotilde and Comte? Indeed they need scarcely wait for Comte's death, since no one ever had less doubts of his own future glory or put more satisfaction, into anticipating his own posthumous existence. "This solemn eternization of a noble marriage might occasionally be awarded in advance, should the true organs of public sentiment judge that it is adequately deserved." We may well believe that these true organs, dependent on their High Priest, will have no hesitation in solemnly declaring him the eternal widower of Clotilde. They will hesitate the less because "the past furnishes us with several spontaneous examples of such solidarity, between Dante and Beatrice for instance, or Laura and Petrarch." Why not Comte and Clotilde too? Yet in fact no one of these three immortal couples was married, and it does seem a little embarrassing that the three most illustrious examples of eternal widowers should all be infractions of the positive law of monogamy. Comte himself is ready enough to recognize in principle that you can only be a widower of your wife. "These exceptional cases," he wrote, "can give no just notion of this new institution which would seem thereby to be restricted to eminent anomalies." For once, Comte could hardly have spoken more clearly; but we are not to suppose that this scruple prevented him from adding a third still more eminent anomaly to the other two. For Dante's Muse was nothing in comparison with Comte's. "My own career," he declared, "will, I hope, present an even more conclusive example than the moving study of union built up by the gratitude of the Western world between Dante and Beatrice." And, still more illuminating: "the personal claims" of Clotilde "to public worship will soon be acclaimed as higher than those of the beloved Beatrice."

Inevitably so, for however high he raised Beatrice, Dante had never made her the subject of adoration. She was not his God, she was not even the Blessed Virgin. Thanks to Positivism Clotilde could become both the one and the other. She could easily take God's place, and even had the advantage of Him, since He did not exist and she had existed, or rather she was still existing, more fully than ever as part of the Great Being. As to taking the place of a virgin, above all a virgin mother, this was more difficult for a woman who was no longer a virgin and had never been a mother. But the expediences of dialectic are inexhaustible. Ever since Clotilde's death Comte had ceased not to pray to her daily in the words of Dante's invocation to Mary: "Virgin Mother, daughter of thy Son." To make this prayer applicable to his Inspiration, he worked out a problem the elements of which he brought from some distance.

It must first be asked of Positivism to establish the fact that a woman can become a mother without ceasing to be a virgin. No miracle was needed for this, as long as you are able to foresee, as Comte did with remarkable shrewdness, that parthogenesis is a scientific possibility. For equally scientific reasons Littré refused to follow Comte along the road of his hypothesis of which he clearly perceived that the source lay in Comte's passion. Littré himself took risks in scientific questions for scientific reasons only, whereas in letting himself be guided by his love for Clotilde it is quite possible that Comte was scientifically correct.

We must not forget the unfortunate Lucie, removed from all honorable intercourse with man and unjustly deprived of the joys of motherhood. On this subject the philosophic imagination of Comte took fire. What an injustice! What a scandal! Must it be said that woman, the object of Positivist adoration, should be eternally tied, in order to become a mother, to those male instincts which of their nature are most unruly? Woman is certainly the most aesthetic element of society: our instinct of the good owes to her its first impulse, but women initiate us even better in a feeling for the beautiful, which they are equally fitted to feel themselves and to inspire in others. "Their appearance manifests to us simultaneously every land of beauty, not physical only, but intellectual and above all moral." This is Comte talking like Petrarch, but his hymn to "feminine ascendancy" reached a conclusion foreseen neither by Plotinus nor Plato. A day would doubtless come, he declared, when, with man steadily developing in chastity, woman would do without him in giving birth to the children she longed for and carrying on the human race. As to the family, it would be all the better for this change. "Thus purified, the marriage union will undergo as definite an improvement as when monogamy ousted polygamy. The Utopia of the Middle Ages will be fulfilled and motherhood united with virginity."

Even if it were merely Utopian, this idea would be a salutary ideal, but from 1854 onwards Comte offered it as more than Utopian: "A bold hypothesis which may be realized by human progress," although he did not feel obliged to say when or even how. But he became very precise on what exactly might happen "if the male organ contributes towards our birth only after a simpler stimulation derived from its organic purpose, one may conceive the possibility of replacing this excitant by another or several others, to be used by woman at her choice."

May then the happy time soon arrive when woman, independent of man even in her "physical functions," will exercise her "affective functions" with total liberty. Protected henceforward "from the caprices of an unruly instinct, the repression of which has hitherto been the chief peril to human order," woman alone will have the initiative in procreation, and we may count upon the nobility of her nature to make use of it for the greatest good of humanity. Comte always regretted that his father had had anything to do with his birth. This strange combination of filial ill-feeling and adoration for Clotilde leaves one speechless. As Poil de Carotte says, "Everybody cannot be an orphan." But if everybody could be born orphaned at least of his father, that would be a step in the right direction.

It must be added that in this mistrust of the male, Comte's own self-judgment was by no means flattering. He asked himself how a young man who had fished his wife up from among the street girls of the Palais Royal could have made himself worthy to become the father of a son of Clotilde de Vaux. To this question he had found no answer. But he was convinced that, sad at having no children and unable to re-marry, Clotilde would have been enchanted if an electro-mechanical shock could have taken for her the place of the defaulting father. She had been virgin mother in her desires. She had therefore been a virgin, and now immortal she still was all she had ever been. Comte aspired to be eternally the widower of a woman he had not married and of a mother who might have had children without his assistance.

Compared with a union of such quality Dante's and Beatrice's becomes, we must admit, a small affair. It is generally agreed that Comte owed to Clotilde the transformation of Positivism into a religion. Littré definitely reproaches him for thus deviating from True Positivism, and with this verdict John Stuart Mill agreed. This could be discussed at some length, for we must not forget that Comte had been the disciple of St. Simon, whose doctrine gave birth to a religion without much help from Clotilde or from any other Muse whatsoever. What is quite certain is that Comte's love for Clotilde speeded up his train of thought towards his "chief philosophical conclusion, the final systematizing of the totality of human existence around the true center of its universe: affection." Already, even before the death of his dear one he had, in his letter of March the 11th, 1846, made clear that it was by this element that Positivism was to surpass in its results all the religions known to us.

Moreover, was not Clotilde the object of a ritual established on Good Friday, April the 10th, 1846, repeated on April the 6th, 1849, and again on August the 26th, 1855, December the 25th, 1855, and Good Friday, April 10th, 1857? All through these commemorations and outpourings, the key dates of their love come up, their exchanges of affection, their vows and promises, marked out by the refrain of two Spanish verses, "Hence my passion is a holy thing. Death has made it divine"; but punctuated also by the lines in which the dead Beatrice calls Dante to undying joy, by Petrarch's two sonnets to Laura: "*Qualpaura ho*" and "*Dolci Durezze*," and by tender farewells to the woman he had loved so dearly, "*Addio la mia Beatrice! Addio Clotilde! Addio Lucia! Addio quella che'mparadisa la mia mellte, Addio!* Farewell little sister! Farewell dear daughter! Farewell chaste wife! Farewell, holy mother, Virgin Mother, daughter of thy Son, Farewell!" And all these invocations, Comte himself explains, are directed to his patron saint "personifying Humanity."

The philosopher was very far from keeping these daily prayers for his private use or leaving the religion of Positivism on the outer fringe of his works. The *Système de politique positive* is preceded by a lengthy dedication to Clotilde, and its fourth volume is completed by a "Final Hymn" preceded by two lines from Dante, "My heart is not great enough to return you grace for grace," followed by that other line, "Virgin Mother, daughter of thy Son" and then by a quotation from the *Imitation of Christ*, "May I love Thee better than myself and love myself only for Thee." Having first assumed the role of Beatrice and next of the Blessed Virgin, Clotilde is now replacing God.

The degree to which we are living inside the story of a Muse becomes nowhere clearer than in reading the dedication to Clotilde: "To the sacred memory of my beloved for all eternity, Clotilde de Vaux (née Marie), who died in my presence April 5th, 1846, at the beginning of her thirty-second year." For if the text for the hymn was taken from Dante, that for the dedication was borrowed from Petrarch. "This life of ours is beautiful to look upon, yet how quickly we may lose in a single day what years were spent in gaining." Again, three stanzas of the *Divina Commedia* bring a final tribute of homage to the Lady in whom are united "mercy, piety, splendor, and all that is great in creation." Nor was this all, for being so deeply engaged in an affair in which the philosopher and believer of "positive religion" was inextricably mingled with the lover, Comte would hardly resist the temptation to write poetry himself. What is the use of having a Muse if you are not going to become a poet? Happily for us he did resist.

Actually this is rash judgment, for it is imprudent to pass

condemnation on verses that were never written. It has been said above that Comte often chooses his words badly, but there are poets whose prose lacks art. What we do know from a sure source is that he had conceived the idea of a mighty poem on *Humanity* for which, if not himself qualified to write it, he was awaiting an author. An Italian poet it must be, like Dante or Tasso, for it seemed one of the Positivist functions of Italy to give to the modern world the epopee of which it stands in need. But Comte was uneasy about this, for after all, who could sing the praises of Humanity better than its High Priest?

Behold him then at work, sketching the plan of this monumental work, "an epic without parallel which will set its seal on the conclusion of the Western revolution just as Dante's incomparable composition inaugurated it." Without parallel, then, except for the *Divina Commedia*—for this time too the subject is a journey, not through three worlds but through the phases of history. It is even to be a two-way affair, a round trip, based on his own three months of descent towards fetichism and this three months' climb towards Positivism, when in the course of a mental crisis Comte swiftly descended and slowly re-climbed the ladder of sociology. It dealt, in fact, with something as different as possible from the cut-and-dried, one-way journey which was all that theology would allow Dante. An introductory canto, three cantos on the descent, eight on the climb back and one final canto to be written later when Humanity should have entered on the definitive period of its story. For the final canto—necessarily static—we must wait for that future, which alone can call it forth.

Meanwhile, the genius of Italy might well bestow upon us the other twelve. And yet... and yet... surely he who has thus outlined the plan of the work is also best fitted to write it. Is it so inevitable that the poet should be an Italian? Comte too is a poet after his own fashion. His heavy prose is adorned with occasional verses which appear to please him mightily:

> *Conciliant en fait, inflexible en principe*
> *Pour composer des lois, il faut des volontés*
> *Entre l'homme et le monde il faut l'Humanité.*

He himself certainly did not think of *Humanity* as being made up of verse of this type—lines which he quite correctly called "systematic poetry," but he certainly fancied, to the sorrowful amazement of Littré, that his career might find its consummation where so many others take their rise: in poetry. To begin with, he owed it to Clotilde. "The fond task fulfilled so admirably," he wrote, "by Dante towards Beatrice is even more deeply incumbent upon me, arising as it does from far superior obligations." For what was Dante's Muse compared with Comte's? Through her the High Priest of Humanity could say in his turn: "*Incipit vita nova.*" To Clotilde he owes a second life, his religious life, and the time appears to have arrived for him to enter upon a third, even should he never complete it.

"Having progressed normally from my philosophic foundations to my religious construction, I must now exceptionally complete this by that poetic creation which alone can obtain for it universal ascendancy." And then, addressing himself to the shade of Clotilde, Comte adds, "Renouncing all vain effort, I hope nevertheless to be able to complete our volume by a sketch in thirteen cantos about that second life, which it explains in me through thee."

This *Vita Nuova* of Auguste Comte in thirteen cantos would have been no slight matter, but how fascinating is this world turned inside out. It is natural that a poet should want to find a Muse, that he may write, but to want to be a poet because one has already found a Muse is a much more uncommon thing. And here it is happening under our very eyes.

One single element in this story helps us to construct the whole. At the time when all this was happening the stories of the Muses were well-known, and Comte could hardly help copying, even if he did not intend it, a drama already played twice before by eminent actors. The memory of his great predecessors haunted him to such a degree that he ended by constructing in Clotilde's honor a couplet made up of a line of Dante and a line of Petrarch:

> *Quella che'mparadisa la mia mente*
> *Ogni basso pensier del cor m'avulse.*

Clotilde is a synthesis of Beatrice and Laura: so how could Comte *not* become a poet? At least we must admit that the philosopher has brought off rather a neat trick in creating this philological monster, for it is poetically valid, and is moreover a marvellous condensation of the essence of poetic Platonism—

> *She who emparadised my mind*
> *Plucks from my heart every base thought.*

This expresses, to use Comte's own words once more, "the angelic ascendancy," which he can "only characterize by combining two admirable lines destined for Beatrice and for Laura."

Once more death in its coming has fulfilled its purifying office. The philosopher will never become a poet, but he has gone through the whole cycle of poetic experience minus poetry: the ideal perceived in feminine beauty, passionate desire, the Muse's refusal of herself, the moral ennoblement of the lover through the virtue of the beloved—all culminating in the transfiguration of the beloved by a death that leads the poet from art to religion.

The founder of Positivism summed up his complete philosophy of history in these words: "Man is growing more and more religious." This is true certainly of his own history. But even when the Positivists rejected the Positivism of Positivist Politics and Positivist Religion, he saw their rejection as religious too—he saw the schism as a battle between the City of the Devil and the City of God. The two armies faced one another under the leadership of angels of wickedness and of goodness: Madame Comte née Caroline Massin, against Clotilde de Vaux.

"The war will go forward under the banners of two women, the green and the red, the dead virgin and the shameless woman who is still alive, the angel who is eternally aged thirty and the demon who has just reached her fifty-first year." The dead Clotilde has entered upon that subjective existence in which one grows no older, but on Comte himself as on his demon wife time still does its work. When writing about his Muse, filial "images" now throng upon him. It is more as father than as frustrated lover that our man of genius—superhuman in his power of work, good, sincere, naive, and a little odd—speaks of her whom he wanted for his mistress. If to be a poet it sufficed to have a Muse, Comte would have left us the greatest epic in the world's literature and Dante's fame would grow dim beside his. But actually he never really quite succeeded in taking his own vocation as a poet seriously. For this fact gratitude is in order: re-reading Clotilde's poems and those of the kindly Charles Jundgill, published with admiration by Comte, one can only ask whether he could distinguish between the poetry of Dante or Petrarch and the doggerel verses of St. Valentine's Day. Clotilde was not to blame, for the most beautiful and best-loved Muses cannot set the well-springs of inspiration flowing in a brain that lacks poetic genius. It was for another task that Comte had chosen her: and that operative female presence which the ear can detect in Wagner's music or Baudelaire's poetry, the mind can detect in Comte's philosophy.

VI. The Muse Who Wanted to Be a Poet

No one whose memory goes back far enough can open the *Souvenirs* of Georgette Leblanc without living over again the opening night of *Ariane et Barbe-Bleu*. We were overwhelmed by the music, yet uneasy and even a little jealous that so much beauty should be offered us by a different musician from the composer of *Pelléas*. And how different was Ariane herself from the exquisite Mélisande we had known. Georgette Leblanc moved gracefully on the stage, acting her way, not without art, through an appallingly demanding role, which her voice could hardly carry. Rumors circulated in the lobbies of the Opéra-Comique. Dukas, it was said, had yielded, against his better judgment, to Maeterlinck, and Maeterlinck had yielded, against his, to the actress—she was set on playing the part—to whom he could refuse nothing. We were furious with them both, but chiefly with her. Could she not have sacrificed her petty vanity for the glory of such a masterpiece?

But there was too much we did not know. How could we have guessed that the woman we saw playing Ariane believed herself to be the third author of the play, indeed in one sense the primary author? We were sorry she should be acting Ariane, but for her Ariane was acting Georgette Leblanc. How could another take her place?—Ariane was Georgette. Was it not her words that had suggested to the poet the very subject of this "Quixotic rescue"? That "incomprehensible, even slightly absurd" woman who delivers captive princesses and, rejected by those she has delivered, "goes off unresentfully to continue delivering," was herself. The heroine was there on the stage: what actress could represent her?

Today we know the story, and it takes us straight into the heart of the drama. Georgette Leblanc never measured the distance between life and art, between being the heroine of a novel and writing the novel, between having an idea and creating the dramatic masterpiece which utters it on the stage. These are two sorts of action with no necessary link, two different orders of idea with no common denominator, so radically different that nothing in the one is any kind of preparation for the other. The soil does not do the sowing. The hero himself has no rights over the work inspired by him. Shakespeare, if he met Julius Caesar, could say with absolute truth: "I owe you nothing."

However different they may be, the Muses have this in common: they do not choose their poet, they are chosen by him. We need not conclude that it could not possibly happen the other way round, for nothing is impossible in the life of the spirit. But there is one serious reason for doubting whether the Muse can choose the poet without peril for them both. A self-chosen Muse only too easily wants to be a more active collaborator than her function as Muse allows: she will not be content just to be there and let the artist do the rest. She will interfere in the work, fancy she had some share in its birth and claim rights of origination—which, in the most acute cases, comes very near to being rights of authorship. Obviously it is not pleasant to find oneself relegated to the rank of occasional cause, and when the Muse herself makes claims for the recognition of her usefulness the artist is in for trouble. Dante placed Beatrice in heaven, but he never said she had written the *Divina Commedia*. From the moment the Muse claims rights over his work, other than those recognized by the poet, irreparable misunderstandings arise and the time is come for them to part.

It all began with Georgette Leblanc reading Maeterlinck's preface to the *Essays* of Emerson. It was love before first sight, for she had never seen him. When the lawyer Edmund Picard introduced them in his drawing-room in Brussels, the cry broke from her, "How wonderful! He's young." They had hoaxed her by telling her he was old, but she was not greatly concerned with his age or his appearance; she was not even looking for the author of *Pelléas* or *Trots Soeurs Aveugles*. Maeterlinck's spirituality was of the earth, but from his soul to hers a thread had been thrown, a knot tied which she would never agree to untie. Was it love? Undoubtedly, but it was something else besides: a "religious experience" of a sort, arising from a total gift of self and the sense of a complete spiritual communion. "I discerned," she later said, "a bent of mind, a vision, thoughts, even a self answering to my own hidden self. I had not tried to find out what he was like, or his manner of life. Between myself and him no barrier could exist. I had staked my life on a solely spiritual issue."

It would be a fatal mistake to question the only evidence available for the interpretation of this story. But Georgette too made a fatal mistake in imagining that two beings are necessarily in tune because their ideas correspond. Through his work we know an author only as author, and that only while he is actually writing. This means that we know the best of him, and he is wisest who rests content with that. Which is Wagner—the man who had it in him to write *Tristan*, or the horrible little creature in a night-shirt who ran shrieking down the corridors in a hotel because his neighbors kept him awake? Not one of the women he loved, least of all Cosima, failed to discover what it cost to live with a man of genius. Both these "beings" are real, and we cannot categorically deny that at bottom they are one and the same, but they do not live their lives on the same plane. Two young Flemings may love beer, good meals, comfortable armchairs and muscle-building sports, but only one of them wrote the preface to Emerson's *Essays*. You may prefer him to the other, but it would be a dangerous error to fancy that he spends his life writing that preface. From time to time he writes something like *Pelléas*—and so being his best self, he will not be yours, for that is the time of all others when his one wish is to be left alone to write. And the ultimate sin that a deluded admirer can commit is to believe he has rights over the author's work and to tell him so. From that moment all is over—or rather it becomes plain that nothing had really begun.

"To be food and fire for his spirit" was at first her sole ambition as she moved from being his Inspiration to being his lover. She did not even have to wait for the physical fulfillment of the affair before catching a glimpse of what lay ahead of her. Here they are in their first journey to the Isle of Walkeren: "It was barely nine when we reached the hotel. I saw myself holding poetic converse with him until sunrise. I rushed into my room, threw the window wide open and pushed a little love-seat into the opening. But he, though he knew what I desired, appeared to hesitate and stood in the doorway. To my empty phrases he replied 'Yes,' 'No,' 'I don't know.' The words sounded like a reproach. I had a desperate feeling that I was making him suffer." One of the things a Muse should know is that even a poet may want to go to sleep.

Everything can be learnt, but the learning takes time. Neither her heart nor her mind was above the average; but when she looked back later at the beginnings of her love affair she saw the meaning of it with complete insight. To a friend who advised her to find consolation in literature she replied, "Don't speak to me of writing! If you only knew how literature sickens me. It is the root of all my troubles. For him as well as for me literature was the primary evil of our union: it falsified our judgment. I understood nothing, saw nothing, was blinded by the sublime on paper." Nothing could be truer—except, perhaps, the fact that if literature had not brought them together there would have been no union.

For the whole story starts at Concord whence Emerson the Sage emerged to preach his spirituality of the daily round to the people of Massachusetts. How could he have foreseen that a young Fleming would presently fall in love with "his novel, natural, persuasive optimism"? Still less could he have foreseen that a young French actress would be overwhelmed by the revelation of that natural mysticism, in which Pascal himself could have discovered no abysses to skirt. "At bottom," Maeterlinck wrote in his preface, "our only life is in the reaching out of soul to soul: and we are gods without knowing it."

It is certainly possible that a secret dialogue from soul to soul has sprung up between me and the farm girl of whom I have just asked the way, a dialogue as intimate as between two people in love. But the world of spiritual relations would be uninhabitable if we insisted on bringing our bodies into it as well as our souls. The girl gives me my direction, she passes on, we each go our own way. It is all nice and tidy. But would it be, if the farm girl were an actress offering me a love seat in the corner of a hotel bedroom?

Our Muse seems indeed to have gone at it with all her heart. "We must live," she had read in that revealing preface, "for no man has the right to hold aloof from the spiritual events of the weeks as they go their dull way. We must live, for there is no hour without its private miracles and its ineffable meaning." Georgette Leblanc—no farm girl, after all—thought she perceived in herself the means of transfiguring any number of the dullest weeks: and just here her mistake began. She did not realize that the spirituality of the commonplace, if it is to be available daily, must be fed at all the sources. To draw endlessly from one well is the surest way of exhausting it. Moreover, she was not even content to be there as a well when he wanted to draw water. She did not realize that a poet must be free to choose among the precious things offered him and that they lose their value if the offer is too continuously urged.

Bernard Grasset's preface is not the least curious part of the volume of her memories. Georgette Leblanc does not seem to have expected it, and she was later (in *La Machine à Courage*) to repudiate it indignantly. Not that it was wholly false, but she could not allow that her twenty years of free union with Maeterlinck rested, as Grasset declared, on a love which did not really have "a man as its object." How self-confident must one be to register such a judgment—and how improbable that it should be so. Maternal love certainly bears a part in every woman's love for a man, still more if he gives her no child. And even if the love of an Inspiration is directed towards the work she inspires, this does not prevent her loving the man who is inside the genius. The real problem arises when these two loves are both fully alive in one person—if the reality of one or the other is in doubt, there will be no conflict. In this case Georgette's love of his work, which preceded love of the man, tried to outlive it. And, to repeat, as a Muse she was insufficiently unobtrusive: she thought of herself as an active collaborator, when the poet only asked of her to be his Inspiration by existing.

Our Muse shows a priceless simplicity when she, his lover, writes, "Because he is not at work he has never been so nice to me in the common sense of the word." What on earth is the other sense, and how can a writer find the time or the temper to be "nice" when he is working? At such a time you can't touch him with a pair of tongs, still less offer him ideas, even on a gold plate.

But we must realize that the poet himself, all unawares, helped to create the ambiguity. He wanted nothing from his love except the fruitful exaltation she really brought, and he overflowed with expressions of gratitude into which his Muse read the recognition of a debt he had never contracted. When Petrarch told Laura he owed his poems to her, that delightful woman had no more illusion of having written them than had Madame Sabatier of being the author of Baudelaire's. But when Maeterlinck wrote in 1895, "I can never reiterate strongly enough how much you have taught me," Georgette Leblanc believed him. She paid no attention to the preceding lines, in which the author had told her, as delicately but also as clearly as possible, that she had taught him nothing he did not know already. Before even he had known her she was the "unknown center" of his being from which flowed, despite himself, "all that was good." What had her love actually brought to him? The certainty that the wisdom of which his writings spoke was a reality. Henceforth incarnate for him in "a being of life and light," "the most utterly alive that had ever existed," the persuasive optimism of the "good shepherd of the early morning in meadows wan and green" took an aspect infinitely more pleasing than in the rather colorless prose of Emerson. But all he asked of her was to play for him, to laugh, to sing, to "leap about in the grass." Georgette Leblanc was perfectly willing to dance in the grass, but not to do nothing more.

Her first great disappointment was *Aglavaine et Sélysette*. Georgette, so she believed, was Aglavaine, and indeed Maeterlinck had meant her to be. But the story ended with a defeat for Aglavaine, which Maeterlinck admitted the heroine would not have brought upon herself had she really been Georgette. Thus the poet's work had yielded to its own inner necessity, had refused to bow before the Muse and had ended as it chose to end. Aglavaine, he complained, had thrown him off the track. The "new woman" he was attempting to introduce into his cast failed to drive out the little Sélysette, "sister of Melisande, Maleine, Alladine, at home therefore in his mind"—and obviously the object of his affection. If Aglavaine was to be Georgette, Sélysette must be happy—which meant that she in her turn would no longer be Sélysette. For it was a defeat: "My grief was deep. Aglavaine's defeat and Sélysette's death filled me with anguish." She desired to be the Inspiration not simply of a masterpiece, but of one made after her own image and likeness with herself on the stage—or, short of that, at least something that she could imagine as being brought to life by her own spirit.

"How I loathed this Aglavaine whose birth I had brought about and for whom I was responsible…I wept as one can only weep at twenty over the failure of an idea." To read these lines is to feel both sympathetic and despairing. From this time on, she tells us, Maeterlinck "escaped from his symbolist fogs and futile little miracle-plays." This may well be, but the author of the Emerson preface had long had within him the power to effect this escape. He had enjoyed the clear light in which the gardens of Concord are bathed during those heavenly days which are the last of summer or the first of autumn. Georgette Leblanc was assuming a responsibility the full extent of which she did not measure but which in fact was not hers at all.

I will pass over, as of no bearing upon our inquiry, the

passionate love affair. It was much broken into by her theatrical engagements and the partings necessitated by them. She laments over these as a lover, not realizing how valuable they were to her. All this is in the ordinary run of such relationships—what is unusual is that the Inspiration herself tried to be a writer. She gave Maeterlinck a manuscript on "the morality of happiness." He read it and told her with exquisite politeness, "You have all the talents, only you don't know the trade." How refuse to believe him, she asks, how avoid feeling a joyous ambition? Perhaps by weighing more carefully the exact meaning of that terrible "only." For a writer who lacks "only" knowledge of the trade, clearly lacks something necessary, and that element of the necessary which is most arduous to acquire.

She certainly did not lack courage, but she had one element in her character too strongly marked for her success: a terrifying truthfulness, which she always practiced in living and which she confused with artistic sincerity. To be truthful in one's work is not the same as being truthful with oneself. The end of these two sorts of truth is not the same, and one often demands that the other be sacrificed to it. When phrases from her letters got into the speeches of Aglavaine and Méléandre, Georgette Leblanc sincerely believed that she was the author—as though there was any connection between a dialogue on the stage and bits and pieces out of letters. Still less could she distinguish between a phrase as written by her in her own context and what it became in the context given it by Maeterlinck. Liszt knew what Wagner owed him because he was Liszt: also because he was Liszt he knew that Wagner owed him nothing at all. But when Maeterlinck said to Georgette Leblanc, "I am stealing from you, am I not?" she took him at his word. But why did she not take literally the words of another writer she quotes, "As usual I have gathered unaware great treasures within you." Yes, surely it was in her he had gathered his treasures, but it was he, not she, who had gathered them. For this reason precisely Maeterlinck had the right to spend them without an accounting.

There is no reason why a writer should not quote the words of his Inspiration, as long as she does not consider herself a writer too. If she is an author and is quoted, then the author's name must be given. When in *Le Trésor des Humbles* Maeterlinck quoted Georgette he would write, "an aged philosopher..."; "an old friend..."; "some wise man or other..."; or he would simply put quotation marks. Georgette Leblanc, having stood this as long as she could, asked him one day why he did not name her as the writer of her own sayings. Maeterlinck replied, "But don't you see that would be absurd! You are an actress...a singer...no one would believe me...it would be ridiculous." Wounded to her very soul, the Muse was silent, but she never forgot.

If language has never led you astray, you may blame the victims of these misunderstandings. Georgette Leblanc inevitably believed that her poet was telling her that he blushed over the actress who sang *Thaïs* "in a sleeveless dress, hands without gloves, waist without corset." To her, it seemed that in his eyes "all this was incompatible with thought."

Clearly she was mistaken here, for he had in fact borrowed her thoughts and had quoted her as he might have quoted Marcus Aurelius. The problem was a totally different one. It was not for Maeterlinck but for the public that Georgette was an actress, and as yet only an actress. The question posed for an author was supremely one of literary tone. It would be difficult to quote in a row Socrates, Christ, Plutarch, Cato, and Georgette Leblanc. At a pinch one might quote a phrase of Georgette's and attribute it to Ruysbroeck the Admirable, but one could hardly back up Ruysbroeck's spiritual authority by Georgette's. Today it would not be easy, around 1900 it was impossible. Nor would it have been entirely just, for after all when quoting Ruysbroeck, Maeterlinck is the author of one book quoting the author of another, while in quoting certain thoughts from Georgette he was drawing out of her writing what she had been incapable of drawing out herself for the construction of a literary master-piece. The power of selection, a good half of what constitutes a writer, was not exercised by her but by him. It is in the works of Maeterlinck, not in those of Georgette, that Georgette's phrases will go down to posterity.

All this she never understood, which is why this very intel-ligent woman ended by being so unhappy. Towards 1897 she began to protest against the smothering of her own personal-ity. She actually glimpsed the danger this might mean for their love, but once on the fatal slope nothing could stop her. The love she bore Maeterlinck, anyhow as she conceived it, should have progressively guided them both into perfect self-realization. This was quite a legitimate view, only by it love becomes no longer a gift but a contract. Maeterlinck agreed and offered Georgette "to publish nothing for seven years," so that she might have the time to bring out her own book. She had the sense to refuse this, but not without making another mistake much more dan-gerous than the one she had avoided. He was offering her time to write her book just as though she had not already written it. But it was there already, on the point of publication—but under Maeterlinck's name alone when it should have carried hers also!

Maurice Leblanc demanded on his sister's behalf a public acknowledgement of her collaboration. He wanted their names put as joint authors. "Maeterlinck answered that the public must not be let into the secret of their private life." This was certainly a reason, if not perhaps the best reason. Georgette compromised by agreeing to a dedication for which Maeterlinck, wishing to be both just and truthful, found the greatest difficulty in choosing his phrases. Georgette gives us the words without appearing to have weighed their meaning accurately. What he wanted was to tell the world that in a certain sense he owed his work to her, but that *qua* writer he was the sole author. It was not an easy thing to say, and whatever way he said it one could be quite certain beforehand that Georgette was in no state to accept it. It is all the more interesting for us to weigh his phrases because, by endeavouring to speak quite truthfully, Maeterlinck has defined the exact limits of what the most deeply indebted artist owes to his Inspiration. The first sentence tells us everything. "To MADAME G. L. I dedicate to you this book which may be called your work. A collaboration nobler and more actual than that of the pen is to be found in thought and in example." To speak of Wisdom he had, in short, merely to look at Georgette and to listen to her: this living wisdom had been always before his eyes.

Need it be said that Wisdom was not at all satisfied? She was certainly touched, but she had expected something different. She did not want it said that "she might be called" the author of his book. The flattering collaboration, "nobler and more actual," with which she had been honored did not console her for the denial of the humbler collaboration of the pen. Nothing in fact can comfort an author for having his title as author contested. This is exactly what Maeterlinck did in 1898, and even more completely when he later suppressed his preface. "It is the only thing he ever did," Georgette was to write, "that was a sin in my eyes." This seems curious, and anyhow we are dealing with an order of things in which the notion of sin hardly belongs. At worst it would be only a sin against sincerity. Maeterlinck, trying to appease her, had written in his preface: "It was enough for me to listen to your words, for my eyes to dwell upon you as you moved through life, for they dwelt upon the movements, the gestures, the ways of wisdom herself." Could Georgette have really believed that this was true?

Poor Wisdom: there she stood, looking at quite clear words and not realizing that the only perfectly truthful ones were those which were refusing her what she wanted.

"That dedication was just," she was later to write. Undoubtedly, but with poetic justice—for all she had given would not have been *enough* without the poet. From the moment when the Inspirer declared herself the collaborator every sort of confusion became inevitable. Faced with the misunderstandings that his phrases might have kept alive, the poet may very well have thought the injustice would be in letting them stand.

There was nothing left now but for each to follow his own path until the day when it would break upon them that they had long been separated. "I decided," Georgette says, "to go on writing for my own satisfaction, and I thought that, giving up only the vanity of publication, I could continue to work and to make progress." But who stopped her from publication? If she could write *La Sagesse et la Destinée* on her own, who forbade her to publish it? She might easily have discovered in the beginning that an author only writes to be read, just as a man only speaks to be heard, but the years passed without enlightening her. She did not understand why the author of *La Vie des Abeilles* was ambitious of putting Fabre "into beautiful French." Yet her contribution to *La Sagesse et la Destinée* was less than Fabre's to *La Vie des Abeilles*. It's a beautiful thing to be a bee, but a bee does not write books.

What a revenge—or better, what a lesson—for her, if she had been capable of understanding a few years later the comic element in Maeterlinck's wrath, when he wrote to *Le Figaro* of wanting a "sensational failure" for Debussy's *Pelléas*. It was, he said, no longer his play—and how true that was. Debussy's *Pelléas et Mélisande* was no longer his, it was theirs, while as to the music, apart from the idea of transforming Maeterlinck's play into a libretto, the work belonged wholly to Debussy.

But Georgette never understood. She did not sing the part of Mélisande, but it never occurred to her that by singing it she would have deprived us, or rather deprived the masterpiece, of Mary Garden's share. She sang Ariane without grasping the reasons for her semi-failure. The question was put by Mirabeau to Lugné-Poe: how could she play the third act of *Monna Vanna*, seeing that it would present difficulties even to one whose métier was tragedy? Georgette answered, with her habitual disarming sincerity: "Certainly not by my talent, for I am entirely ignorant of the art of tragedy...but I can give you the answer today, dear Mirabeau. I shall play it with all the power of a devotion and a love which only once, and only in one man's eyes, found their reflection."

But tragedy, alas, is the same as literature. The tragedian's sincerity does not belong to his life but to his art. When she consulted Mounet-Sully he suggested three years' schooling, but the play was to appear in a month and she could not wait. When she consulted the older Coquelin he understood her immediately. "You love him? He loves you: you love one another! Well then, act with your heart."

The extraordinary thing is that in the event Coquelin proved not entirely mistaken. Georgette did act with her heart, and as she describes it, "The technical difficulties became apparent to me step by step as my perception grew." It was sad for her that the technical difficulties in being at once Muse and collaborator of a poet did not become apparent at an earlier stage.

For the rest of the story is the commonplace one of a liaison coming undone and the woman trying vainly to remake it. The peculiar element in this one is the determination shown by Georgette Leblanc to maintain her rights as the initiator of the whole affair! "I am sure I am prematurely worried, but it was I who first conceived our love. By this act I accepted responsibility: I watch over it, provide, forestall." She might as well have said that all was over. When the poet presently married "there was nothing left for him to destroy of what had once been." Ariane could at least find in herself one last consolation, that she had played through to the end a part which even in the theater was never mere acting. Once more she had essayed a "Quixotic rescue."

We no longer possess the *Carnets intimes* of Georgette Leblanc, which is a great pity, but the *Souvenirs* tell us, no doubt, all that she considered essential for our understanding of the problem. Even *La Machine à Courage*, so necessary for anyone who would understand the real nobility of this quixotically generous spirit, does not contribute any really new element to our special inquiry. She did not have to tell us that the "hateful introduction" which Bernard Grasset printed without her authority at the beginning of the *Souvenirs* could never win her approval. One does not see what introduction could have pleased her; indeed it is clear to every reader that she did not want any. One feels too that her inflexible will would certainly not have yielded after her first defeat.

She stood firm, never disowning the love she had known, never for an instant lowering herself by cursing it, but also never renouncing her ceaseless effort to understand the meaning of her own story. She seems to have arrived at this, to some degree at least, when she wrote two years after the disaster some short notes on suffering, jealousy, and passion of which she speaks like a noble animal who rejoices to have experienced them. After which it is no surprise to read what she has to say about "mutual understanding." But it becomes abundantly evident that what she had told us about Maeterlinck: "there are in him two people," was equally true of her and that she made the mistake of wanting to fuse them into one.

"From the first," she writes, "I fell into the error of confusing the meeting of minds with love." At twenty this mistake is venial, but in Georgette's case it took the rather unusual form of mistaking understanding for love rather than love for understanding. We must not forget that it all began with that preface to Emerson's *Essays*!

"I fancied that nothing could unite two beings more closely than to share the same ideas about poets, painters, scenery." True enough, but the very reason why that "chemical affinity" which spells love, and even day-to-day friendship, are on such utterly different planes that to seek in them a transcendent spiritual understanding is a useless quest. If success had been possible, she should at least be paid the compliment of our belief that no human being could have deserved it more.

And yet one must admit that Georgette was incorrigible. At the very time of return upon her own past, at the moment itself when the clear distinction between love and understanding is forced upon her mind, our "deliverer" asks herself, "Could I have got along with d'Annunzio, that man of magic who fell out of his window through excitement?" It must be admitted that she had the common sense to say no, but for a very odd reason. It surprised her that other people did not fall out of other windows from boredom. "As a brief episode he would have interested me, but in the long run I would have been bored to death." This is really first-rate: she does not ask herself for one moment how long d'Annunzio would have stayed with her! No doubt she had Eleanora Duse in mind, but the story which ended in *Il Fuoco* could only have been written once, and it was not Duse who was the first to be bored. "The meeting of minds is no dream creation," says Georgette Leblanc. Yet when she is dreaming about it, her imagination carries her on to the love of one poet or another. In a lordly way she decides that she would not have chosen to do what no other woman succeeded in doing, remain with d'Annunzio.

Her mistake was perhaps even more deep-rooted. As a little girl she had (so soon!) written in her diary: "Great ideas are put on the shelves but not made use of. I shall use them." This is quite frightening. There are excellent reasons for putting certain objects on the shelves, especially if to be made use of is not their purpose. Among them are great ideas which are not there to be used but to be served. No harm that a little girl should make this mistake, sad that this woman high of heart and soul should never have recovered entirely from her initial error. She put too much love into her art to be a very great artist, and too much art into her love to be an entirely happy woman. But who are we that we should judge her, and what sort of man would he be who would fail to pity her? She had attempted the impossible. To offer the artist more than he asks is to refuse him the only help he needs.

VII. The Art of Flight

Can married love be the well-spring of poetry? Coventry Patmore gives positive proof that it can. Can the marriage of a poet and his Muse become a source of inspiration? The marriage of Robert Browning with Elizabeth Barrett should provide material for an answer. Certainly one would like the answer to be yes—partly because of the rarity of the thing, and all the more because, killing two birds with one stone, we could add to our collection that very rare bird, the male Muse. For both were poets, they loved each other, they married, had a son and lived in a state of conjugal bliss which in no way diminished their genius. You cannot re-read their works, placing them chronologically in the framework of their lives, without being entranced by this moving love story, but is it really the story of a Muse? It would seem not: when Browning married Elizabeth under the romantic circumstances so well known to us, she had published a great deal and was already the author of the *Paracelsus, Sordello,*

and many other important works. One who was to rank with the most illustrious poets of England married the most famous woman-poet of England, and if one reflects on their mutual admiration before they had even met, one is inclined to think that their poetry had more effect upon their marriage than their marriage had on their poetry.

The *Sonnets from the Portuguese*, in which Elizabeth Barrett turned the story of this love into poetry, is close enough to the reality for us to know by what feelings she was inspired. Six years older than Robert Browning, cruelly tried by sickness, still loveable—for he loved her—this invalid of forty had long lost the bloom of youth. She knew it well: you have only to read *A Denial*. All her reasons for saying no are there, above all this one:

> We have met late—is it too late to meet,
> Oh friend, not more than friend!
> How shall I answer thy request for love?
> Look in my face and see.

When she urged him to marry another woman, younger and gayer than herself, it was not that she might save this poet from losing the Muse she had never been to him. It was simply because she feared, as she admits in Sonnet XIV, that he loved from pity, or for the look in her eyes or for her smile—in short, with a love that might not be lasting. When in Sonnet XVI she declares that she doubts no longer, does she not prove that she had in fact doubted?—not, indeed, of herself or him, but of the security of a future that all human wisdom would have judged uncertain. She married Browning at an age which Petrarch had already loved Laura as his Inspiration for twenty years. On their way to Italy they visited the Fountain of Vaucluse, and Browning, taking his wife in his arms, carried her over the shallow water and seated her on a rock in the middle of the Sorgue. It would have taken more than that to turn our happy pair into a Petrarch and Laura. A happy marriage is not too common, the happy marriage of famous poets is a very great rarity. But a poet happily married is not the same thing as a poet whose inspiration would dry up if one special source ceased to flow.

It is abundantly evident that the happiness Elizabeth and Robert Browning found in their marriage helped their work, but Elizabeth's is not linked with her love for Robert nor Robert's with his love for Elizabeth, as the *Canzoniere* with the love of Petrarch for Laura, or the *Vita Nuova* with the love of Dante for Beatrice. Robert is certainly not absent from *Aurora Leigh*, but the epic is not dominated by him. In it Elizabeth, who had always admired George Sand, gave vent very fully to her reforming zeal. As to Browning, he had been Sordello before he loved Elizabeth, and he remained himself after he married her. She too is present in his work but when he speaks of her he is hymning not a Muse but the happiness of a life spent in the mutual intimacy of the home.

> My perfect wife, my Leonor,
> Oh heart my own, oh, eyes, mine too,
> Whom else could I dare look backward for,
> With whom beside should I dare pursue
> The path grey heads abhor?
> My own, confirm me! If I tread
> This path back, is it not in pride
> To think how little I dreamed it led
> To an age so blest that by its side
> Youth seems the waste instead?

143

Nothing could be lovelier or more genuine than such a poem, but it is called "By the Fireside." Browning measures his happiness. He knows Elizabeth might have refused him:

> Had she willed, still had stood the screen
> So slight, so sure, twixt my love and her:
> I could fix her face with a guard between,
> And find her soul as when friends confer,
> Friends—lovers that might have been.

But he had gained the lover without losing the friend. Instead of a long and unrewarded testing, Elizabeth's heart had spoken the word that filled his own empty heart. But it is his life Browning owes her, it is himself, it is not his art in any direct sense. Elizabeth would later write her ode to *Napoleon III in Italy*. The man called, during her life-time, "Mrs. Browning's husband"—for she was more famous than he—was later to write *The Ring and the Book*. True, he invoked in this poem the inspiration of Elizabeth (I, 1390-1416), for by now she was dead. There could no longer be any doubt that two poets could find happiness in marriage and could draw effective inspiration from their happiness, but they wanted that happiness for its own sake. Elizabeth said yes in order to become Browning's wife instead of saying no in order to become his Muse, and the proof that that was what the poet wanted lies in the fact that he never ceased to be grateful to her. Not every poem requires a Muse. The Brownings would have made a mistake had they married in order to find inspiration in the routine of daily intimacy, but they did marry in order to be happy.

It is when we read the life of Goethe, from that virtuoso in the art of running away, that we learn what the story of the Brownings cannot teach us—how love can be made to serve the higher ends of art! As we have said, there are psychologists who seem to think that no special problem is posed by these stories, that they are only so many cases of what they call "sublimation of the emotions." But it has been made clear (I hope) that we are here concerned with quite a special kind of sublimation, of which neither the origin nor the meaning seems clearly identifiable with other types. They are distinguished by their quality of deliberateness, by being conscious, considered, sometimes even calculated. It may well be—as Petrarch shows—that a poet's may not be at first a poetic love, but it will very soon turn into one. It is surely a peculiar way of sublimating the emotions which begins by cultivating them. Even in this we must anticipate variations, or rather we must accept each case as special. Every graduation may be found, from that quest for a Muse which with Wagner and Baudelaire look at times like a hunt, down to those obscure cases where an artist is following a secret instinct rather than any thought out course. All this wholly different from the medicinal sublimations in which a man obsessed by bodily emotion seeks salvation by a transformation through which comes his deliverance. It is perfectly possible that the contemplative soul may to some extent sublimate the love of a woman into worship of the Blessed Virgin. But it is difficult to see how he could cultivate the love of a woman in order to feed and quicken his worship of the Blessed Virgin. The thing is totally different. If you wanted a prescription made up, you would need a different one for each case.

Goethe in his conversation on March the 5th, 1830, with Eckermann, was invited to compare his passion for Lili Schönemann, just declared by him incomparable, with all his others. Lili had been neither the first nor the last woman he had loved with "true deep love." On reflection he had to admit the fact of these other loves, and that no two loves were alike. It depends not only on ourselves but on the object: "Nor must it be forgotten that a third force intervenes in love, the 'daimonic', which is present in every passion and finds its life element in love." There is nothing like love for helping man to stand upright, "face to face with the daimonic," without which no really great work is achieved in art or in anything else.

Every artist speaks his own language. Goethe christened "daimonic" that power from the outside which works upon a man of genius, works more the more powerfully the greater he is. He must always welcome its action, not wholly abandoning himself to it but directing it to his own purposes. A man, he said, must never let it usurp the ruling power of his will, but he must allow for this force and indeed count upon it. "The daimonic," he said too, "is something that cannot be explained in terms of mind and thought. I do not find it in my nature, but I am subject to it."

Many artists have tried in different words and in their own fashion to say this, and none has ever put it better. Goethe is not thinking of Mephistopheles, whom he described (in his conversation of March 2, 1831) as too negative a being to be truly daimonic. Mephistopheles is demoniac, which is not merely a different thing but the very opposite. "the daimonic manifests itself in wholly positive activity," and even more with musicians than with painters. Goethe had Paganini in mind. Thereupon the worthy Eckermann comments with simplicity, "I was enchanted by all these definitions. I shall now understand with more precision just what Goethe means by the idea of the 'daimonic.'"

No need to upset this placid confidence, but without trying to explain more than Goethe himself could explain, let us hold on to one important idea. The work of an artist, or of any creator in any field whatsoever, depends upon a transcendent and quasi-supernatural power—it does not absolve him from doing the thing himself, but without it he can accomplish nothing great.

It is, according to Goethe, precisely because love is utterly separate from intellect, that the daimonic always enters as a third party between lover and and beloved. In the affair with Lili Schönemann the daimonic had been "uniquely active." Goethe had himself totally under the power of this force. He later said that a man abandons himself to it fully believing that he is following his own desires but actually becoming "an instrument of the power that governs the universe, like a vessel accepted as worthy to receive the divine." We must never forget that in love "the daimonic is in its finest element." Though so many women came after her, Lili remains unique.

Nothing could explain better than Goethe's own words why the pages in *Dichtung und Warheit* dedicated to this muse breathe after so many years the very breath of youth.

"Poetry it was that perfected in me the sentiment of love experienced in youth." From the first the *truth* in his love had been *poetry*. Nothing was lost if he could rediscover poetry.

Perhaps it was a mistake to say that nothing goes deeper into the problem than these words, for there are those other words of his in reference to his sister. She was a woman of the highest morality with no element of sensuality, for whom the thought of giving herself to a man was hateful: she married and never ceased to suffer from having done so. "And because she was unhappy even with the best of husbands she vehemently dissuaded me from the union with Lili that I had planned." Did this sister perhaps know Lili too well—or her brother? Lili Schönemann, who was later to become Madame de Turckheim (in 1778), never seems to have felt any aversion towards marriage—even with a banker. Frederick Soret states from "authentic documents" that she was ready if necessary to follow Goethe to the United States in order to marry him. Read again the poet's words, reported by Soret in his *Notice sur Goethe*, "Yes, I loved her as much as she loved me. There was no unsurmountable obstacle—and yet I could not marry her! This affection had in it something so exquisite, so intimate, that it affected my way of writing on the details I have given: when you read them you will find nothing there the least like the ideas of love that are propagated in the novels." It is easy to believe this, and perhaps this is just what his sister realized before he did. You do not marry that element in a woman which has an influence on your style, yet that was the element that Goethe loved. Congratulations are in order to both of them on what his biographers call "the first flight, away from Lili."

This was not to be his last affair of the kind, and it is the very last that will always be the most interesting, for to it we owe the immortal *Elegy of Marienbad*. It is impossible to re-read without a smile the story of Goethe putting down a pair of candles in front of Eckermann, giving him this jewel to read and asking him what he thought of it. Of Eckermann's rather confused impressions the most external are by far the more important for us and most worth recollecting. "The lines," says Eckermann, "were written in his own handwriting, in Latin script, on strong parchment and fastened with a silk cord into a red morocco cover. The very outside revealed that he attached more importance to this manuscript than to all his others." Truth to tell, this talisman was more in the nature of a reliquary. It contained the mortal remains of the violent passion which the marvellous old man had just experienced for a child, the young Ulrike von Levetzov.

The story is well known: the first meetings at the baths of Marienbad, the visits, the innocent conversations between this charming old gentleman and the young girl—who was a hundred miles from suspecting what was happening. Followed the proposal, which with anyone but Goethe would be deemed farcical, and Ulrike's refusal. She was seventeen, he was seventy-four. This time at least, Goethe had not taken to his heels. It was his last chance and he must have known it. At his age there could no longer be the old question of freedom to be jealously guarded!

After Ulrike had refused him he fled far off, so deeply upset that he became seriously ill. But even in the diligence which was carrying him away forever from his last love he was feverishly composing the *Elegy of Marienbad*.

In the sixth series of his inexhaustible *Approximations* Charles du Bos translated this moving masterpiece with detailed comments. It must have especially attracted him, for he was not much given to discussing anyone he did not care for. With this episode Goethe became in his eyes, probably for the first time, fully worthy of being loved. It was a beautiful story. Charles du Bos's literary olympus was reserved for the spiritually exalted, and there was an element of bourgeois banality in Goethe, both as man and artist. It was only tardily that Charles du Bos admitted this solemn old fogey with his walking-stick and his watch fob into the ethereal company of Shelley and Keats—not to speak of Claudel, who must have started for the door when he saw Goethe coming in. But here at last was the *Elegy of Marienbad* to win forgiveness for everything. In this adventure Goethe himself saw an "unforgettable turning-point in his life," and we may see his life's supreme point of enlightenment; for here Goethe arrives in a world which owes nothing to art but to which art owes so much, the world of religious spirituality.

We must not exaggerate. In his very interesting book, *L'Education Sentimentale de Goethe*, Robert d'Harcourt has made it clear that Goethe did not wait for Marienbad to become open to the "temptation" of religion. He even believes him to have had a mystical crisis lasting about two years (1768-1770), with illness playing a larger part in it than love, all the more because perhaps the illness was the one best designed to disgust a man with love. But it is also for this reason that the two happenings cannot precisely be compared. At the beginning of his first "conversion," if it may so be called, Goethe was a foolish fellow regretting his follies, and above all the heavy payment he had made for them. He had been suspicious of his intellectual calculations and was thinking of prayer as "good business which brings in returns." The only thing that corresponds to this religious Philistinism is the series of reflections about love that resulted from the totally unexpected experience of his engagement with Lili Schönemann. How very pleasant it was! And what a good bargain he had made! For Lili was a twofold personality. Her grace and her charm belonged to Goethe; the worth of her character, her self-confidence and the strength of judgment which she showed in everything, all this was her own and Lili would certainly continue in possession of them, but not without advantages for her husband. "I observed all this, I examined it and rejoiced over it as over an investment the interest on which I would be drawing to the end of my life." There is no summit that Goethe did not reach, even the summit of platitude.

We must do him the justice to say that nothing of the kind mars the Marienbad love affair. Charles du Bos was right in saying that this time at least, a little late but not too late for his renown, Goethe had made the most splendid of his discoveries. How stupefied Ulrike must have been, when later she read this immortal elegy, to discover the role inarticulately offered to her by this "M. le Conseiller." He might, as she one day remarked when she was politely keeping him company at the waters of Marienbad, "have been her grandfather."

"I can doubt no longer! She steps forward to the gate of Heaven, she lifts me in her arms. It is thus I was welcomed in Paradise, as if worthy of a life of everlasting beatitude. Nothing more to pray, to hope, to long for: I had reached the object of my most secret strivings. The contemplation of this unique loveliness dried up my tears of longing at the very source. She gathered me in as if I were worthy." There has never been a better example of how little credit a Muse deserves for a lavish bestowal of her gifts.

Perhaps these were all clichés. But when considering Goethe as a poet, this unreserved surrender to the hackneyed is an absolute guarantee of sincerity. He might have said this a hundred times before he reached the age of seventy-four. What happened is simple enough. To Goethe in his turn had come a flash of that elementary reality which nothing can replace, and because it was the same for him as for all the rest he spoke quite simply, as they did, of a child's face that gave him a glimpse of Paradise. He felt it, of course, so powerfully chiefly because the gates of Paradise had just shut upon Ulrike, leaving poor Goethe outside, enriched only by the memory of that last kiss which meant so much to him and so little to her. Goethe must have been very unhappy indeed to quote Scripture! It was, however, the Epistle to the Philippians that the poet invoked to tell us into what bliss he was plunged, not by the grace of Christ but by the sight of Ulrike.

"The peaceful serenity of love in the presence of the beloved is comparable to the peace of God which, as it is written, surpasseth all understanding. In this the heart finds its repose and nothing can disturb its conviction, the deep conviction of belonging to her." This time he is not thinking in terms of reckoning his capital and investing his money so that it shall bring him in good dividends! This time Goethe is simply making a supreme acknowledgement, of which the importance is all the greater because in his case there is no question of specifically Christian religious feeling, but rather of that spontaneous religious element to be found in the most pagan natural outlook. He verifies what C. S. Lewis was later to say about the images used by God to bring man back to Him since man relapsed into paganism. Goethe writes with complete sincerity. "The purest depth of the heart is shaken by a struggle towards free and thankful self-aban-donment to something higher, purer, unknown. This is what is meant by piety. This happy lifting of the heart is my good fortune when I am in her presence."

The very effort of translating this magic language chases away its music. In abstract words it repeats in poignant fashion the sorrow of the eternal Adam driven from the earthly paradise. Goethe complains of being robbed henceforth of the blessed vision of Ulrike, that intuition of Wisdom on which the memory alone is not enough that he may live. It must be repeated, this philosopher is seventy-four and his Wisdom is seventeen. But man is so made that when he meets beatitude he asks for her in marriage. You may be called Goethe and be past master in the art of timely flight, but the day will come when you are convinced that the only means of taking possession of Wisdom is to marry her.

This time, says Charles du Bos, "Goethe's love, the last love of his life, revealed religion to him: when Ulrike is present she is for him a true Beatrice." Nothing more accurate could be said, and I am glad that it is another man who says it, particularly because he is not considering my special problem. But I am less sure about the distinction, subtle as it is, introduced by this critic between Dante living on the memory of Beatrice and Goethe craving for the presence of Ulrike. Certainly Goethe tells us so himself. He longs to see Ulrike all the time, but surely it is going rather far to contrast him with Dante in this as being a "cardi-nal point in the difference between *categories* in the sense which Pascal gives to the word." Insofar as they are poets, all these men are in the same category, and the Dante who wrote the *Divina Commedia* is apt to obscure the Dante of the *Vita Nuova*. He had to live on the image of Beatrice once she was dead, but while she was alive and while he could see her it was on the sight of her that his happiness was fed. He did not even wait until she was dead to sing her his most beautiful songs, just as Goethe began his *Elegy* in the carriage that was taking him away from Marienbad. The real difference between them lies elsewhere: in the fact that the whole of Dante's art took its life from this unique wound, whereas, after so serious a crisis as to threaten his death, Goethe desired to be cured—and succeeded. Even the glorious angel Ulrike ended by becoming for him a part of the impersonal "eternal feminine" which drew him upwards.

It is really too late to make discoveries in this field, for even at the time of Petrarch the story was a *vieille histoire*. It was so well known that it was told about many poets without any effort to discover whether it had really happened to them. It *must* have happened because they were poets. Who was this Folquet who left Genoa for Marseilles, fell madly in love there with a lady of great beauty, hymned her in his poems and, plunged into despair by her death, turned monk and became a bishop? And who exactly was that Geoffrey Rudel, poet of remote princesses, whose romantic biography as it used to be told in the thirteenth century is a little masterpiece, far better than all his own writing?

It is a short story and singularly complete. "Geoffrey Rudel, Prince of Blaye, was of the highest nobility. He fell in love with the Princess of Tripoli, whom he had never seen, because of the good spoken of her by pilgrims from Antioch. He composed many poems about her, the music of which is beautiful though the words are poor. He became a crusader and crossed the sea, so much he desired to meet her. But he fell ill upon the ship and was left for dead in an inn at Tripoli. They told the Countess, who came to see him in his bed and took him into her arms. And he knew that she was the Countess, recovered his hearing and his sight and praised and thanked God for having kept him alive until he could see her. And thus he died in her arms and she buried him with great honor in the House of the Templars. And then that same day she became a nun from the grief she felt at his death."

Impossible to tell more of the truth in a smaller number of untruthful lines. For the whole of this little scene appears to have been made up by some ingenious reader of Geoffrey Rudel, a romance based on what can still be read in his poems. All the same, everything in it is true with that legendary truth which is sometimes more true than the truth of history. Rudel would not have sung about his princess if she had not been remote. It is easy to understand how he longed to see her, but as soon as he held his Muse in his arms the poet died, because he was a poet. If she had left him first, he would have become a monk like Folquet at Marseilles, or written a theological epic like Dante or penitential psalms like Petrarch, or like Goethe discovered rather late the meaning of the word piety. All these stories, if they are not strangled in the beginning through some folly, find their end in religion or in some substitute for religion. There is no question of this element being introduced by the bystander. The difficulty would lie in leaving it out.

VIII. Art and Eros

The mass of evidence we have examined presents us with a strange mixture, in which three chief elements are mingled in unequal and varying proportions: Art, Eros, and Religion. This last element is commonly found only in correlation with the two others; it affects their action and in retrospect throws a light on the meaning of the story as a whole, but the story would certainly have happened anyhow. I shall look last at Religion. It is Eros that lies at the heart of these stories of Muses. It is deeply implicated in the creation of the works of art we have been considering, a sort of primeval energy apart from which nothing would have happened.

We may well ask why this should be. Art is not of necessity linked with love. Out of the immense number of works created by artists known and unknown, I have chosen three or four masterpieces only, whose birth appears inseparable from a great passion. But we must be on our guard against a false impression. These are exceptional cases, and it is for their individual significance that we are examining them. However few in number, these masterpieces at least seem to have been conceived in love—for their authors as for ourselves, their existence seems inseparable from it. In their regard I put the problem: is there a profound relationship between Eros and the creation of certain great works of art?

But is it in fact possible thus to delimit the problem? Directly you enter the domain of art, questions become of that universal character which belongs to the very idea of art itself.

A masterpiece is first of all a piece of work, and the greatness of certain such works does not entitle them to be classed as a species distinct from other artistic production. Why, after all, does the artist produce? Or, if it seems better to narrow the scope of the question: why does anyone write? A contemporary essayist asked himself with surprise when he was framing this question whether he was not the first to ask it. Perhaps he was, at least in such a universal and direct form, but it involved him in perils which he did not seem to have foreseen. For it is possible to discuss brilliantly and at length the reasons that drive a writer to write, on condition that you search for them in some other direction than art. An author may write because he wants to be talked about, or to earn a living, or to spread certain truths, combat certain errors, fight for the triumph of certain causes. Nobody will deny that motives such as these have inspired much that has been written. But it is not certain that, even in cases of this type, they explain the primary fact that certain men have chosen writing as the means of reaching these ends. There are other ways of earning a living besides writing books. Poets especially could easily find surer methods. As to various kinds of propaganda, apostles would rather speak than write, some of them act more than they speak, and when writers are found among them, a special vocation alone can explain the choice which they have made of this method of propaganda. Doubtless also you will find among them some who have devoted themselves to the service of a cause only because it gave them something to say. The writer most wholly given to a cause is still primarily a writer.

A confused realization of this fact explains perhaps why the question has so seldom been asked: why does one write? For when the question is asked for its own sake there is only one possible answer: a man writes because he wants to write. A young man knows that he will be a writer before knowing what he is going to say or even whether he will find anything to say. After his first book has been published he often knows the anguish of an author driven by the need to write but whose sterile brain can bring no book to the birth. The reverse is equally common. We have all known men with heads full of ideas, sometimes new and often interesting, who express themselves easily, sometimes even elegantly and forcefully, but who are prevented from writing down anything by a sort of "stylophobia." You say of these men, "He talks like a book." But they seem able to talk their book endlessly without ever writing it. The answer appears so frivolous that, because they could think of no other, many people have felt it was wiser not to ask the question. All the same it is the true answer. There are people who cannot see a piece of wood without pulling a knife out of their pocket to carve it with; others, again, cover any bit of paper they get hold of with endless drawings, not in order to picture anything but for the sheer pleasure of the moving hand which gives birth to lines. This is not enough to make an artist, but no artist exists without some primitive urge of this kind and no writer exists without the urge to write. At bottom the scribbler is a genus of which the writer is only a species. This too is why the writer is always a man of action while he is writing, even if he is a metaphysician or a contemplative mystic when he is thinking. It is no justification for writing that one has yielded to the itch, but a man who never feels the itch will never write anything.

Many people write with nothing to say, just as others draw to quiet the fidgets in their hands. But to paint a canvas is quite a different matter, and to create a work of literature is not to be confounded with the pleasure of blackening a piece of paper. It is not even necessarily a pleasure, and the word necessity, although it fits better, can only be applied with precision to one moment in a complex operation. When language is needed to describe the genesis of any work of art or literature, it seems today to borrow its metaphors spontaneously from the various phases of animal reproduction. There are "fruitful" and "sterile" authors, to say nothing of minds so sterile that they will never be authors, however much they long to be.

But the same artist can go through phases of alternate fruitfulness and sterility. To escape from a sterile phase he must "conceive" the idea of a possible creation, seeing the main lines though not as yet clearly enough to undertake its execution. One talks at this stage of the "gestation" of the work as though the artist were carrying within him a living seed, then an embryo which grows, develops and becomes perfect, all as it happens with a pregnant woman. The time of gestation is not in this matter determined as with physical birth, it varies according to the man and the work, but there must be such a period and its limits are not really arbitrary. Just as, according to the proverb, an honest woman does not bring her child into the world before nine months, so too the true artist does not hurry the "birth" of his work until he feels it to be viable. Neither too soon nor too late—and it is an art in itself to know how to choose the moment for birth, that the work be not an "abortion." But when the time has come it must be born, and although these are pains of another kind, they are rightly compared to the pains of childbirth. Some works are born easily, others in long anguish. When his fruit is ripe the artist must expel it from within him. Other reasons for writing, or the question of knowing "for whom you are writing," are relatively unimportant. This could not be better expressed than in the words which Fromentin puts into the mouth of Dominique. "I told you a while ago that I felt within me stirrings of a will, not to be somebody, which is meaningless, but to produce, which seems to me the solitary excuse for this poor life of ours. Grasp clearly that I write not to increase my dignity as a man, not for my pleasure, not for my vanity, not to profit others, not to profit myself, but to expel from my brain something which is tormenting it." It would be hard to convey better that the artist when his time has come feels the need to be delivered of his child.

This artistic process from pregnancy to delivery recalls the similar process, described for us by Socrates, in the field of thought. Art is not the only domain in which the natural history of the intellect is comparable to that of the animal. All knowledge is the fruit of an act of conception by the spirit, even the driest knowledge of all, which we call a "concept." Yet we know nothing of scientific Muses, and even the one we saw presiding at the birth of a new philosophy was called upon to intervene only at the moment when the heart's needs were rebelling against the primacy of the intellect. There must be a reason why certain great works have been conceived in the love of a man for a woman to such a point that their birth seems as natural as the birth of a child. What is the relationship which can explain this marvellous symbiosis of Eros and Art?

Once more Socrates comes forward to set our steps on the right path—or Plato rather, for it is of the Socrates of the *Symposium* that I am now thinking. There is absolutely no end to the thoughts arising from this work—in its lovely clarity one may fail to realize its profundity. The homosexuality in it is disturbing, but we must not be mistaken about its bearing. I do not mean that it is unreal. It is only too real, and the statement that the wise man must rise above it to reach real wisdom shows plainly that, although a low step, it is yet held to be a first step on a road that leads to wisdom. The fact is not to be denied, or even precisely apologized for, but understood, that we may draw the right lessons from it.

These are not always the lessons it is alleged to teach. Certain homosexuals misuse it, as though Plato had taught that their practices were the chief source, or at least a necessity, for great art. The problem is far more complex. It is indeed with "Greek love" that the *Symposium* is concerned. But Plato teaches that while it is good to experience it, it is evil to yield to it. Here, then, is a case analogous to those with which this book is concerned. The passion of a man for a man is noble and salutary only when it is overcome and used as a force urging the lover upward to the intelligible world. If there is one Greek whom Corydon cannot claim, it is certainly Plato. First of all, Corydon is a devotee of the cult vowed by its adepts to the "Aphrodite of the people," of whom the philosopher thinks no good. Then too, and not by chance, Corydon is a pederast, whereas the Greek love Plato has in mind is directed preferably towards young men or perhaps even to youths, but never to young boys, still less to children. This passion ought to direct the lover towards a true philosophy, and what can he hope for from a friend who is too young for mind to answer mind? When Corydon confides to his private journal that he hopes to fornicate, he is not inventing any new temptation, but he is excluding himself in a twofold fashion from the companions of Socrates, he is not the man for Plato's banquet.

At the distance dividing us from the Greeks it is impossible to recapture the exact meaning of their words, above all on subjects where we are not certain we even understand those of our own contemporaries. Were it possible to do so it would be wiser to abstain. If we lack that wisdom, and must try to find our way in this labyrinth of feelings remote from our own, at least let us not assume too easily that we have succeeded. Let us take—as a plain statement, which may help us on the way of understanding—the remark of Pausanias in the *Symposium* that the Eros of Aphrodite Pandemos, the popular Aphrodite, "is interested in women as well as in boys." There can be only one meaning for this strange juxtaposition—it matters little whether man's desire is directed towards a man or towards a woman: as long as it is looking for fleshly satisfaction, it is equally low. It would not, I imagine, misrepresent Pausanias' meaning if we said that the homosexual Eros is more damaged by this promiscuity than the heterosexual, for it is normal that man's passion for woman should be fleshly, and it is just because it is natural that this love is dangerous for the philosopher. Through a curious paradox its very abnormality seems to invite homosexual love to seek a meaning outside the physical relationship which in this case is meaningless. Pausanias suggests this: the lover who expects from the man he loves what others expect from the woman plays traitor to Aphrodite Urania, the heavenly Aphrodite, in favor of Aphrodite Pandemos just as they do, but without their excuse.

Without claiming to be certain on the point, one may ask whether, in the eyes of Plato's Pausanias, this does not give homosexuality an advantage over ordinary love. Those who turn towards woman, he says, "only have pleasure in mind and are not concerned with integrity." This is a society in which a woman could not be the object of a spiritual love, nor therefore the wellspring of nobility and goodness which she became in the Middle Ages. It never occurred to anyone that love of a woman could be motived by any other desire than natural physical pleasure.

Why then be astonished if in Plato's mind it was unnatural love that prefigured with surprising closeness what courtly love of the twelfth century was to be? This sublimation of homosexuality does not, of course, make it normal. But by forbidding all physical satisfaction he lifts it into a different order from fornication, and in so doing bestows upon it a new meaning.

Those who follow Aphrodite Urania, the celestial Aphrodite, by seeking out young men, unlike those who run after women or boys, will love "the most generous and the most virtuous even if the less beautiful." Far be from them that evil love of the body, as impermanent as its object—for the body withers and dies but "the lover of a beautiful soul is faithful all through his life." This love is as eternal as its object. Celestial though it be, this love is still a passion, for there is nothing the lover will not endure to please the beloved—no trial, however senseless or cruel, that he will not undergo, no achievement he will not attempt, to become worthy. Phaedrus had already said it before Pausanias: there is nothing like the thought that his beloved is watching him to inspire in the lover "shame of evil and eagerness for good." Here, as later on in the courtly love of the Middle Ages, a whole system of ideas and feelings is closely linked, which in various ages and under paradoxically different forms tend spontaneously to reappear as a totality.

Because we find in the love of the *Symposium* the same mingling of flesh and spirit, the same utilization of the longing for a beautiful body and a beautiful face through which to rise up to intelligible beauty, this analogy becomes of interest in discussing our own problem. Art is not actually involved, yet we can count upon Plato to suggest in a single phrase what love can make of art when art is there: Plato himself is at once Phaedrus, Pausanias, Socrates, and even Drotima of Mantinea, from whom Socrates claims to have learnt that the object of love is not beauty itself but "the giving birth through beauty" with the hope of self-survival. Everyone strives to survive his earthly life as best he can. Some do it through the body, and those are the ones who turn by choice towards women, for "their loving procreates children, thus assuring their own immortality, the survival of their memory, happiness in a future which they picture as eternal." But the others, whose fruitfulness is of the spirit, to what should they give birth? Wisdom, answers Drotima, "and the other virtues whose fathers are all the poets and those artists also who possess inventive power."

How illuminating this is. These subjects do not lend themselves to actual demonstration, and dialectics have no foothold here. But a kind of metaphysical imagination offers glimpses of real connections between facts of an order apparently widely different. Poets of every sort working in stone, in color or in sound are ceaselessly in childbirth—more truly than the philosophers. They must conceive, carry their fruit, and give birth exactly as though some mysterious affinity linked art with genetics. And this may really be the truth. It is possible and on the whole probable that the creative fruitfulness of the intellect lies very near to biological fruitfulness, and that production may be a special case of reproduction. Or maybe it goes the other way, and in a being like man in whom the work of the intellect is the supreme act, physical conception may be only a material and inferior participation of the body in the fruitfulness of the spirit. Whatever be its interpretation, this connection is enough to establish the stories of Muses as parts of a whole that gives them meaning. Love as a passion accompanies and intensifies art. It even seems its natural concomitant, giving us to think that physical fruitfulness, with the profound vibration that it brings to the being it stirs, helps, encourages, and feeds the fruitfulness of the intellect.

This idea cannot be dismissed, but we realize that in trying to state it with exactitude one encounters hosts of difficulties. The most obvious one is that in this matter what is against nature in the order of flesh seems natural in the order of spirit. The Muse seems to render the poet fruitful, the musician also and even the philosopher. It is the male who conceives, carries the work within him like his fruit and finally brings it into the world. But here appearances are deceitful, for we must not forget that the artist chooses his Muse and loads her with the fruitful energy from which he hopes to benefit. It is really he and not the Muse who conceives the future work, for there is no case ever noted in which the woman loved by the artist has transmitted to him by spiritual insemination the germ of the work that was to ripen within him. Petrarch, Baudelaire, Wagner, conceive on their own the creation that one day they will give to the world. Nobody imagines that Beatrice ever suggested to Dante the *Divina Commedia*. It really is a question, as Baudelaire put it, of spiritual hermaphrodites, and every hermaphrodite involves a male. He fertilizes himself, and his Muse if he has one only inspires him with the ideas that were his already.

To get an exact idea of what the artist expects from his Muse, it is helpful to meditate on the experience of the troubadours. Critics are agreed upon the importance of the word "delight" and of the feeling conveyed by it. It is not the function of a poet to define, and states of the soul, not being "things," do not in any case lend themselves to definition. But to make clear what the word for a feeling signifies, one can appeal to the experience evoked by it: the "delight" of the troubadour is the pleasure inseparable from certain moments of interior exaltation. That is the element it has in common with all joy, as distinct from mere enjoyment or pleasure—an agreeable feeling but much more superficial and, for the poet, of a widely different order.

Of delight or joy it may be said, as of pleasure, that each man takes it where he finds it. The troubadour's joy is different from other men's both in the springs whence it flows and in the end it is seeking. Its most obvious well-spring is nature, so persistent a theme in Provencal lyric poetry that critics have noted regretfully the repetition that so soon turned it into mere cliché. Many poems certainly do open by hymning the spring, but this is not true of them all, and it is important with poetry to be on one's guard against mistaking lack of originality for lack of sincerity. The basic themes of lyric inspiration: love, death, nature, match those universal experiences which each of us lives anew. Commonplaces for the race, they are new for the individual. And all these stereotyped openings suggest at least that the troubadours saw their delight as intimately linked with the delight of nature bursting into new life in the springtime. The song of birds, the blossoming of plants, running streams, are but the outward showing of that inward delight which disturbs alike the earth and the poet. For nature is herself a poet; and, if the birds are heard so continuously in the descriptions of spring which are the delight of the troubadours, it is because nature through their notes is achieving that perfection of poetry to be found in singing and in musical measure.

The first theme leads on almost inevitably to a second. Those birds whose songs are loveliest, above all the nightingale, sing only when they love. At the highest summit of nature's spring intoxication is found love and the delight it gives. Listen to Geoffrey Rudel:

"When the nightingale in the bosky wood gives love, asks for it and receives it, when his song is heard of joy and of delight, when his eyes are ever upon his mate, when springs are clear and meadows smiling and a fresh delight holds sway, then comes deep joy and dwells within my heart."

The fullest well-spring of delight is man's love for woman. It is too the most abiding, for it does not at all depend upon nature or its seasons. As long as love reigns in the poet's heart, joy too is there and song springs forth:

"Nor rain nor wind stop me from making poetry in my dreams, the cruel cold kills neither song nor laugh. For love is leading me, and my heart is held in the perfection of natural happiness: love nurtures me, guides me, supports me: love alone gives me joy, alone gives me life."

In these words Peire Rogier expresses admirably what so many troubadours have repeated to the point of wearisomeness: the inexhaustible well-spring of delight is the love of a poet for a woman. Others, such as Rambaud d'Orange, also perhaps faintly bored with the spring, profess to have no other source of inspiration:

"I sing not about bird or flower, frost, snow, or heat. I sing not nor ever have about delights of this kind, I sing only for the lady to whom my thoughts take wing, the most beautiful in the world." Clear as this is, one discerns the end of the poet's joy even as one discovers its source—for its end is song.

We are now, you will think, facing a difficulty admitting of no solution, a tangled skein which cannot be unravelled without getting mixed up with various others—the problem of the interpretation of art in general and of poetry in particular. The main misunderstanding separating artist from art critic and art historian is rooted here. Artists think that what historians, critics, or professors talk of under the name of art has very little relation with what they themselves are doing. This is not the place to discuss the question for its own sake. In any event, it may well be that the answer must differ, or at least be modified, in reference to different epochs, artists, and works. There are artists like La Fontaine whose aim has been to teach and who have still remained great artists. There are artists whose aim has been to analyze the passions, describe manners, teach an ideal of living—and some among them have achieved it as great writers, Racine for instance, La Bruyère, and Rousseau.

Because of this, historians of art in general, and more especially of literature, are naturally drawn beyond the work of art in search of what it has to teach either about mankind in general or about the ways and manners of a given period. I have no wish to stop this, but only to offer a caution sometimes neglected. Just because the writer is a writer he cannot be the perfect mirror of his age. The desire to write, which means the desire for public self-expression, is enough to mark him off from his ordinary contemporary. This is still truer when the writer has chosen to be an artist and is working consciously to express himself in a work that is beautiful. But my caution applies supremely to those works where the author had no aim save to give pleasure, to be an artist. It must be granted, at least as a hypothesis, that the work itself is one of the artist's aims. In certain very special cases, perhaps the purest examples of artistic creation, the artist's whole aim may be fulfilled, totally expressed in the work itself, so that the thing created and its significance are one and the same, it has and needs no purpose beyond its own existence. All this means that a poet may pour back into his art all that he has to say: the feelings he is expressing find their real meaning only in the work he is creating, to the degree in which that work is their consummation.

Without wishing to reduce courtly love to a mere poetic theme, a formulary that, even where it fits best, would still be inadequate, we cannot doubt that the troubadours often made use of it as a means towards the end of art, which was what they were actually pursuing. The delight they talked about endlessly and cultivated with so much care was supremely that emotion from which sprang their songs. Nature too offered them inspiration, but none comparable with this. "All around me," said Geoffrey Rudel, "I find in plenty masters and mistresses in the art of song: the meadows, orchards, trees, and flowers, the songs of the birds, their trills and their plaints in that fair and gentle season in which I find so little delight. For no entertainment can bring with it the joys and solace of a noble love."

Bernard de Ventadour's saying must be accepted to the letter: "The sole business of my life was to love joy, and in joy my songs took their rise." If he sings better than the other troubadours, of which he has not the smallest doubt, it is precisely because his song is born of joy. "Poetry has no worth in my eyes unless it comes from the bottom of the heart—but it can come from this source only if perfect love is reigning there. This is why my songs are better than the others, because my whole being is filled with the joy of love: my mouth, my eyes, my feelings." Even a troubadour not so certain that he sings better because he loves better than the rest is still quite convinced that he sings only because he loves. "Joy" or "delight" is so dear to them only because it is what makes them into poets. "I take pride in my endless loving and longing, for it has often plunged me into dreams and brought me to mastery of song.... For the wealth I joy in I thank that dear and lovely being to whom I send my song, even more, if it be possible, am I grateful to love."

This general experience does suggest with all simplicity that poetic fruitfulness is closely linked with the fecundity of nature. Even in our artificial civilization, overloaded as is its spirit with theories and doctrines, the artist may sometimes rediscover the immemorial secret which birds pass on to one another, season after season: love that you may sing—not the first platitude to be charged with meaning.

The troubadours made a great discovery, perhaps the most important of all their contributions to the art of poetry, when they observed that birds sing only in the spring but that humans can be in love all the year round. What matter the wind, the cold, and the rain when the artist has spring eternally in his heart? The well-worn saying springs into one's mind—"Woman, summer everlasting! Woman, immortal spring." The phrase may not be worth much, but we should always remember that authentic human experience is what commonly gives rise to such clichés. The troubadours sang of "joy" or "delight"—and it is certain that with them at least this is one of its meanings and the deepest. It meant that creative exaltation experienced by the poet in the yearly fecundity of springtime, made lasting by the permanent fecundity of love. It is the *mundus muliebris*, the world whose atmosphere Baudelaire saw as essential to the birth of great art.

The oneness, or at any rate the close connection, between all these things is seen not by a logical process, but from the fact that the intellect itself is a living thing and there is no iron curtain between the body's biology and the spirit's. The entire man longs and loves and, if he happens to be an artist, creates art. The desire to beget through beauty is an urge of the entire being. This joint energy works both ways, for the creator pours into his love as much of art as he puts of love into his art. This is what makes of their symbiosis a unity wherein the nature of the various elements is profoundly modified. There are artists, even among the greatest, to whom the in-mingling of sensuality seems unworthy of art as they conceive it; but the contrary is more generally true. For, the artist never desires this in-mingling for the sake of love but only for the sake of art. It is love that receives a mortal wound in these conflicts. Love, which can only conceive itself as an end, finds itself reduced to a mere means.

Mathilde was too intelligent to be deceived by Wagner's most frenzied transports. It was not she whom he loved, even in *Tristan*, it was *Tristan* he loved in her. She was merely Isolde's understudy, whose part she was playing in Wagner's studio. It is hard to find the right word for a sentiment of this nature, for the poet and his Muse are not just play-acting, or, if they are, the ardor of their rendering is such as to deceive themselves. Sincerity is the right word, as long as we remember that all the sincerity in these stories is for art, not for love. After all, Wagner himself died of old age, without having ever leaped off the balcony of a Venetian palace. The only victims of this drama were Tristan and Isolde. They really did die of love, and so exquisitely that they have outlived both author and model. They will live to bury many future generations of interpreters and spectators.

If we accept Baudelaire's suggestion that a great artistic creator has an element of the bisexual, the fact still remains that he is by sex a male. Dante, Petrarch, Baudelaire, Wagner: and curiously enough, if one were considering what other names to add to these, none of them would be a woman's. I hasten to add that I am speaking only of the past: what the future holds, who knows? It may prove that social conditions inhibited woman's creative powers, or at least offered her too unfavorable a field to give her full opportunity of exhibiting them. One often hears this urged; and it is plausible if it is not wholly convincing.

Since education for women has become general, women of considerable talent are to be found in all branches of art and letters, and it seems strange that none of them has reached the highest peaks. With so many women musicians why no equal, I will not say of Bach, but of Mozart, or even of Chopin? The very emotions of women seem to need male musicians to express them. In letters it is otherwise, where the existence of specifically feminine genius cannot be contested, that is to say a genius of which the vital force itself is feminine. The letters of Madame de Sevigné, *La Princesse de Clèves*, *La Vagabonde*, could, only have been written by women. Yet it may still be asked whether the very femininity of these works is not what, after all, places them in a different rank from the *Divina Commedia* and *Tristan*. After all, Nature usually dowers the male with the finery and the songs in which her art is found. She has not done this for man, but she has given him the power to do it in her place. And is it certain that the genius of the artist is not obliged, for the creation of his most moving works, to have commerce with Pan and the forces he symbolizes, forces which in man find the high point of their flowering in love of woman and the mystery of fruitfulness that envelops it?

It is wiser to go no further. To compare, said the scholastics, is not to prove. In this matter there may *be* no explanation, discoverable here below, anyhow. Best, perhaps, simply stop at setting down the facts. The conclusions of the psychoanalysts and metaphysicians when they get on to these problems rather support this feeling. C. G. Jung in his *Essays on Analytical Psychology* presents the sexual problem as the mere opening "of an infinitely deeper question before which its importance grows pale, that of the *spiritual* relations between the two sexes." He goes on to say that "woman's psychology rests on the principle of the great Eros which unites and separates, while man has always been linked with the Logos as ultimate principle. We can translate the concept of Eros into modern language by *spiritual relationship* and that of Logos by *objective interest*." Applying this distinction to my own question, which is not the same as Jung's, I would say that in nothing is objective interest more evidently paramount than in the production of a concrete work designed for a spiritual end, an end foreseen and willed—and this is what art is.

But in saying this one does no more than explain differences of function already well known by creating names for each. No advance is made by saying that "woman as Inspiration" results from a "projection" of the *anima*, whose nature is "erotic-emotional"; because, even if this is true, it does not tell us why this subjective projection should sometimes appear to be needed for the birth of something as objective as a work of art. And can it be necessary, in order to explain what the images thus "projected" have in common, to discover underneath the erotic fancy dress "obvious fragments of a primitive mentality composed of archetypes which together constitute a collective unconscious"? Plato was a primitive of this kind, and Aristotle accused him of mistaking mythology for metaphysics. But the mythology itself needs explaining, and it would be hard to disprove that every man at every period of history is capable, through human nature itself, of making up these myths all over again, without help of that other myth the "collective unconscious." What is the gain, over comparing the growth of a work of art to that of a child in its mother's womb, if we call it "scientifically" an *autonomous complex*. So is the child, and the bird and the tree. So is delirium at times, but unless you can accurately explain "poetic delirium" you have said nothing on the subject that is of interest. Apart from substituting words for things, science seems to have done very little to enlighten us on the relationship between Art and Eros. We have known since Plato that this relationship exists—like that other, between art and religion.

IX. The Artist and the Saint

To all appearances the way of the artist is seldom a road to sanctity. Some saints are to be met with in literature, but neither St. Theresa, nor St. John of the Cross, nor St. Francis de Sales sought sanctity through practising the art of writing. St. Francis has been made patron of journalists, but one smiles at the thought of his being under contract today to provide copy for one even of our most orthodox dailies—he might not find it easy to reconcile the claims of the devout life with the distractions of the press room. Music claims St. Cecilia, but she is more famous for her sanctity than for her compositions. While as to painting, apart from St. Luke, better known as evangelist than as painter, no single name comes to mind except Fra Angelico. In him we have an undoubted genius and one whose devotion gives its life to his painting, but so fully a painter that the Church, despite his fame as *beato*, hesitates to name him *santo*: yet all his works are miracles! One simply does not expect to meet sanctity on the highways of art.

Yet who can live among artists, today or in the past, without observing how many among them are haunted by religious problems and longing for a spiritual life—it is beyond them, yet dimly they feel a call to it.

I am not thinking of such a musician as Franz Liszt—his life, full though it was of women and of passionate love affairs, was the life of a spoiled priest. He always realized it himself, and the soutane he wore intermittently towards the end of his life was the outward sign that he did. But for his mother and his confessor Abbé Bardin, he would have entered a seminary in 1830. One can hardly blame Abbé Bardin for his prudence. Liszt realized himself that only a special grace from God could have enabled him to live up to such a vocation. "Poetry, music, and also a touch of rebelliousness in my nature have ruled me too long. *Miserere mei Domine.*" May God indeed have mercy on the Canon of Albano! But I must regretfully set aside an over-simplified case of this sort, in which the interior tension drawing an artist towards sanctity found its resolution in works of art in which the sanctity that might have been simply evaporated. We shall understand better what happens in such cases if we examine consciences less awake to the real nature of their problem. Nor do I want to select instances which may appear deliberately chosen to prove my own theory.

The *Journal* of C. F. Ramuz offers an inexhaustible quarry, for this delightful romantic poet analyzed himself deeply and appears to have noticed very early on that the vocation of writer has in it an element of abnormality. "A clergyman," he wrote (December 23, 1896), "studies, passes examinations, and is then provided for by a regular salary." But why does a writer first enter upon a life of endless labor in which success comes late if it comes at all, and then not always to the most deserving? That is the main problem. An artist longs not only for success, but for that infinitely rarer and more precious thing, a success he has deserved. Musings of this kind are not uncommon even with a youth of eighteen, but the conclusion drawn by Ramuz less than a year later (April 7, 1897) moves one to admiration. "Every day I see more clearly what my *vocation* would be, if it were an ordinary vocation to be entered upon lightheartedly like that of lawyer or doctor. I *must* become a writer."

A "vocation," the poet clearly indicates, is often a misnomer for what is in fact a deliberate choice, the result of a preference which would not exclude the possibility of some other. But the writer does not choose, he is chosen. It is another question whether he will have the courage to obey the call, but he has still heard a call even if he rejects it. He knows that this road is the only one on which he will find "the security and happiness of a task achieved and a vocation fulfilled."

What other vocation besides the religious can be compared with such a call springing from the soul's depths? He who hears it feels he is a "clerk" in the meaning given to the word in the Middle Ages, that is to say a chosen being, set apart in virtue of a personal destiny, consecrated not from any initiative of his own to the service of a good which will be his portion and his heritage. He can, of course, reject it, but this rejection will be treason and will be the first step on the road of a life spoiled. "Still painting?" said a friend to the painter Bonnard on finding him at his easel, "Of course," the artist answered, "what would you have me be doing?" What else indeed could one have him do? What else could he want to do himself? Michelangelo was made to sculpt or to paint, just as Dante was made to write. Were they to succeed in something else they would still be failures.

This is why, even if he is paid, the artist's chosen toil is really done free. A man who works as sculptor, painter, or musician merely to get a living is plying a quite honorable trade, but he is not an artist, for an artist will only live by his art if people will agree to buy it just as he has made it. Here lies the great adventure of his life, for while other workmen must make things that satisfy the public taste, he has to induce the public to buy the things he has made to satisfy his own. It is a great deal to ask of a man, for it is by no means certain that the public will discover the value of his work before the artist dies of starvation. And, worst of all, he is never quite certain of their value himself until after his first success. He does not only desire that the beauty he is serving shall be recognized for its own sake, it is absolutely essential for his. For until it is recognized, how can he be quite certain that it is beauty? Only when his first admirers, followed by his first disciples, begin to arrive. Wagner expressed exactly what he felt when, at the banquet following the first Bayreuth performances, he publicly uttered the words reported by Guy de Pourtalès in his *Life of Liszt*: "This is the first man to put his faith in me, the man without whom you would probably never have listened to a note of my music, my very dear friend Franz Liszt."

Yet it is then, in the hour of his first success, that the most subtle temptation comes to the artist, to let the genius that created his public be directed by that public. Once he has won them, they always keep asking for the identical pleasure they experienced the first time. So the painter sells himself to the dealer who is certain he can place any number of copies of the same work with his customers for any length of time. The novelist rewrites the same novel. The musician repeats the same songs. The artist, in short, becomes his own disciple and calls upon his talent to exploit the creations of his genius. The exploitation is perfectly legitimate: *honni soit qui mal y pense*: but from the moment he begins to practice it, the artist becomes the craftsman: the creator has ceased to be.

Am I demanding that the artist should be a hero with abnegation equalling that of the saints? Not so. By what right can we, his public, make *any* demand upon him? It is he who makes demands upon himself, and this is what goes against human nature. Intelligent people do not behave like that, and the artist realizes it and feels himself to be unlike other men. He even begins to emphasize this difference by his dress and his behavior. Subtle changes lead all the way from *Scenes of Clerical Life to Scènes de la vie de hohème*, as if the second were a mere parody of the first, an unconscious mimicry of the "contempt of the world" counselled by all great spiritual leaders, Christ above all. The round, almost clerical hat, the scarf a sketchy likeness of clerical bands, all this fancy dress may really have a meaning. It may indicate another variant of *contemptus mundi*, contempt for the "bourgeois" world and its "idiotic conventions" as young Ramuz calls them, and of the spiritual emptiness that plagues it. The artist does not behave like a sensible man, but how sensible are sensible men? Not very, thinks the artist. It is true that they can always give a reason for their tastes, their behavior and the things they admire, but if you press them, you find these reasons are not their own. Everything in them comes from outside, which for the artist makes them unendurable. "I want to live at a distance from them," Ramuz wrote (June 24, 1897): "The futility of all they do would be in too violent contrast with the gravity of the mysterious energies I must obey, energies purposeful and not to be deflected from their purpose." This youth, called by an inward voice and accepting the call, has exactly the semblance of a soul obedient to grace and amazed by the emptiness and the tumult of the world outside.

Nor is this the only similarity. The writer experiences all the rhythms of the spiritual life and the tides of grace: its uncertainties above all, what the saints call the periods of aridity: "There come times when no thought will come, when the pen drops from your fingers. In vain I struggle to set to work, to gather together my ideas, to set down in black and white what I think is in my brain."

Inspiration is dead, and when grace has deserted him the artist laments those happy hours when everything was clear and plain in the joyous fecundity of genius driven by the breath of the spirit. It is then that he entreats the power whose very capriciousness makes it seem like a free and independent being—a person, in short. Sibelius said one day, speaking of his *Fifth Symphony*: "When the final shape of our work depends upon forces more powerful than ourselves, we can later give reasons for this passage or that, but taking it as a whole, one is merely an instrument. The power driving us is that marvellous logic which governs a work of art. Let us call it God."

Ramuz likewise cannot express his meaning with precision except by borrowing the language of religion: "My abilities are not great; may I at least accomplish the little of which I am capable. This is the prayer I make daily, imploring the unknown. My will is powerless, but there is something stronger than my will which escapes me, yet which can do all things. It is to *that* I pray, I speak to that god within me."

It would be hard to say it more plainly. Whatever name the artist uses—"that," "the unknown," and various others, he is aware that he is directing his prayers towards a God of some kind. What Ramuz writes later (on April 18th, 1915) has the pleasure of anticipation fulfilled: "The artist and the saint are one and the same. Self-sacrifice, world renunciation, acceptance of insult and privation, states of grace, a rule, disciples.... Parallelism of the two mysticisms. To be in God. The truths of the Gospel transferred to aesthetics, so to speak." This tense epitome could be developed endlessly, yet in its clarity needs no commentary. It expresses a personal experience which cannot be denied, more especially as there are others sufficiently like it.

What Ramuz has to say oddly resembles what Oscar Wilde wrote in his *De profundis*: "I remember telling Andre Gide one day when we were sitting in a Paris café that, while metaphysics interested me very little and morality not at all, there was nothing in the teachings of Plato or Christ that could not be directly transposed to art and find there its perfect fulfillment."

It may well be that Gide recalled this remark when he wrote in *Numquid et tu* the lapidary phrase: "It amazes me that no attempt has ever been made to draw out the *aesthetic* verity of the Gospel."

Actually it matters little whether or no he remembered, for in passing from Wilde to Gide (if pass it did) the formula has become more exact. Gide is not thinking of the vague, aesthete's Christ of Wilde, but of himself and of what it would mean for the writer if he could have an artistic freedom as absolute as the freedom of the gospels for Christ's disciples. What could he not write who has left all things to follow art and has sacrificed to it father, mother, wife, and children? For the sacrifice of self for art is not the hardest thing, but the sacrifice of those we love. The obligation of this sacrifice is felt most keenly by those who love best and hence feel most incapable of making it. This was the drama of Goethe, and of Clavigo, whom Gide discovered so many years after he had written in his journal (August 5, 1934): "Interesting and important aesthetically, psychologically, and morally." Yes, and all three together, for aesthetics and morality are here interlocked. Clavigo sacrificed himself only because he had already sacrificed to art all he loved. But Gide had the certitude that he who does not give up all for art cannot enter the Kingdom. You must take nothing with you, cling to nothing, so as to be held by nothing, keep yourself, like the saint, wholly free for the one thing necessary. "Oh, for the coming of that nomad state, for which my whole soul longs!" These gospel aesthetics are very bad theology; but nothing makes more actual the similarity between two experiences that yet are so deeply different—of writers serving their art and of Christians serving their God.

Even if the writers never told us any of this, we should still know; one has but to look at them. The "world" is not deceived, it reacts in just the same way to both kinds of man. It is well aware that you "become an artist" just as you "become a priest"; and there are not a few families in which the announcement of either of these vocations is received with equal dismay. Not that they want to force any particular profession on the young man—or even urge him to "follow in his father's footsteps." Oddly enough, they would agree to any profession whatsoever except one of these two. And the reason is a simple one: "they are not professions."

And this time the world is quite right: they are not professions. For this very reason, if he yields to the pressure around him and enters some profession to make a living until he is certain of his own feelings, the artist-to-be feels as lost and unhappy as the priest-to-be. The one or the other knows no rest until he has left all things to give himself wholly to what he loves. The young Ramuz gave lessons for a livelihood, but he abandoned everything when he realized that in working for a living he was endangering that creation yet to come which was the sole reason for his existence. So too Gauguin, settled in life, married, father of a family, left it all to go to the Marquesas islands, where he died impoverished and alone. Sooner or later the time comes when the words once heard by Dante sound in the heart of every artist: *Incipit vita nova*. From that hour he puts off "the old man" to follow that inward power which summons him to follow, giving no reason. All his faculties are reaching out to the perfection he longs for—seeming so close, yet ever eluding him, to be known only when the work is finished and perfection is there—and at that he may not recognize it.

No one is humbler than the artist before his art, even if he is vain before men. He is even humble about his life, which is, he is aware, different from other lives. He asks by what unmerited grace he should be called from among so many. This feeling goes so deep that when he is among men engrossed by the needs of ordinary life, modesty will not let him speak of his own way of living. He hides it as the saint hides his life of prayer, which can be talked about only among saints.

"I hold myself unworthy," Ramuz wrote (on October 10, 1902), "of functions so high I do not view them as a livelihood, but almost as a priesthood." What priest ever feels so worthy of this priesthood? And it is a priesthood that the poet exercises. "What is called poetry," to quote Ramuz again, "is the sense of the *sacred*, and the need, once the sacred is seen, of helping others to share it. This involves all that poetry deals with, people and things, the lowliest and the highest, for the sacred is everywhere, or it is nowhere at all. All poetry is religious, all poetry is a kind of religion."

This transfers us suddenly into another order of thought, for now it is the object itself of art, not simply the attitude of the writer, that is seen as akin to the divine. The world in which the artist lives, when he is looking at it as an artist, is different from our world. We see everything as so many things to be seen or so many invitations to action, action usually that serves the simplest purposes of utility. The artist sees them differently. Everything he sees is, or can be, an invitation unsought by him to create things more true, more beautiful and therefore more real than the things he sees, hears, touches. Everything, whether sentient or not, he sees as blindly striving to become something which only his art can make it—not a different thing but more fully itself, what it ought to be to realize its being by the total unfolding of the beauty hidden within it. This beauty only the magic vision of the artist can uncover. He sees it capable of more beauty than it has, and longing to be rid of the imperfections that mar it, be transformed into an image wrought by man, in which art has achieved what nature was striving after. This is the artist's meaning when he defines himself as a visionary of the real. This is how the world of art is born which Charles Gounod christened the human kingdom, peopled by a multitude of beings whose ultimate justification is found in the pleasure they bring: pleasure in seeing, reading, listening, with nothing offered to the mind save what makes for that pleasure's fullness.

This is the fashion in which, though in a wholly different order, the universe of the artist resembles that of the contemplative. In this, the contemplative's world, said Pascal, everything is hiding a mystery; in the artist's, the thing hidden is not God, but each thing is the sign of something else, which it already in some measure is, which it is art's function to bring it wholly to be. This world too is sacramental in its own way, since each being is the rough sketch of what it would be if its sole function were beauty.

Plato, Plotinus, Dante, Petrarch, sometimes even Baudelaire, have spoken for a host of others whose work attests the same conviction, where they tell us that the world of nature is but a stammering which the artist is sent with the vocation to turn into intelligible speech. Just as, according to Plato, the "real reality" is not the material object but its idea, so too the true reality sought for in everything by the artist is not what he sees but what he makes. What we call the thing itself is for him only the image of another image not yet born, but so perfect that when it is born it will be the reality.

Ramuz is not alone in believing he has a priestly mission.

It would be useless to look for the least rudiment of theology in Rodin; yet he says, "real artists are the most religious of men." While others live only by their senses, in a world where they are satisfied with what appears, the artist divines the presence of a multitude of hidden forces and things invisible, seen clearly neither by the eyes of the body nor of the mind. "Lines and tints," he goes on to say, "are merely the signs for us of hidden realities. Our eyes plunge below the surface to what lies below, and when we later copy outlines we enrich them with that inner truth."

It is not to be wondered at that every masterpiece should have a quality of mystery, for it really is the revelation of a mystery. True enough, it cannot give this revelation without the mastery of a technique: for one who would practice sculpture in the religious spirit of Rodin, the first commandment is to learn how to model an arm, a torso, a thigh. Yet, all said and done, it remains a fact that "art is a kind of religion."

Rodin is prudent. He does not go so far as to say that art is religion, but he believes that before that secret reality whose presence it is his mission to reveal, the artist is very close to the priest. It imposes itself upon him as an absolute. It does not depend upon him, but he upon it. Humbled before this transcendent reality, what can he call it but God? Everything is religious in those "temples of Art" in which we bring together so many curious objects, of no utility, their significance wholly in themselves. The visitor pays at the door and goes in full of respect. He looks around—as he might listen to a concert—asking for nothing except the delight which he knows will be his. He is in a sacred world peopled with things all the more majestic because they are of no practical utility. Like the transformation of a model into a portrait, there is a sort of miracle of transubstantiation. Art, like love, shows what is called reality to be lying.

All these religious analogies have their effect upon the artist.

He is drawn to think of himself as *magus*, sometimes as a hero in the life of the spirit, even as a kind of saint. But he is in fact none of these things. The truth about the artist is quite different: for his splendor cannot be divorced from a wretchedness that torments him even when he cannot discern its cause. The saint's perfection lies within himself, and he is perfect in the measure of his achievement. *Esote perfecti*: the spiritual man addresses these words to himself, the artist to the things of his creation—be ye perfect. It is in the perfection of his works, not of himself, that the artist finds his fulfillment.

Thus it is that all the quasi-sanctity, all the asceticism, of the artist is for the profit of something not himself. Well aware of this, he knows that like a mother he must conceive and spend his own substance in nourishing the child that is to be born of him. "I am perfectly willing," Gide said, "to have no very definite existence of my own if I can give one to the beings whom I create and draw out of myself." This says the whole thing, and it almost seems as though one had to choose between making a masterpiece, or making oneself (in the sense in which a saint makes himself). André Gide's is one of the most illuminating examples, since he protested beforehand against any interpretations of his work which failed to look at it with the realization that art is its absolute center. Art was the center not merely of his work but of his life. This explains, and in his own eyes most fully justifies, things he would have seen as unfavorable—if he had not found in art, like the Greeks he claims to follow, the justifications of his morals. After all, it is in the beauty of his song that Croydon finds his salvation. But how diverse and manifold beauty is. It is necessary to all its forms, and as one excludes the other, the command is laid upon the artist to identify himself with no one, so that his art may give birth to them all. "It is not himself he is painting, but he could have become what he was painting had he not become wholly himself." But in becoming wholly himself, what *has* he become?—a writer, obviously a fluid being whose essence is to put himself wholly into each of his creations in turn.

"I now hardly know who I am," Gide said, "or perhaps better, I never am at all, I am always becoming." Even in saying this he flatters himself, for his "I" never becomes himself, but always someone else. His "I" is a becoming.

There is a certain magnificence in a man who can thus lose himself in his work. It carries the moral beauty of all sacrifice, but the price paid for it is a heavy one. "You are myself," the artist says to his work in Goethe's *Künstlers Erdewallen,* "you are more than myself: I belong to you." The creator himself is empty, for all his substance has been poured, so to speak, into the being he has begotten, nourished and brought to perfection. Then too, the anguish that torments him between the birth of one work and the conception of another is seen in its true meaning. No chance of deceiving himself, for during his time of sterility he is aware of his poverty. But what would it mean if the artist had kept for himself all he has generously poured out in his works, if the substance so lavishly scattered among his characters had been used in the creation of his own character and personality? Richard Wagner admits us to a secret of enormous importance: "If I did not possess this marvellous gift, this strong power of creative fantasy, I could follow my clear knowledge and the *élan* of my heart: I should become a saint."

Virtual sanctity that diffuses itself among the works of art never becomes a real sanctity. Yet Wagner is not the only man who asked himself this question and answered it in the same fashion. The admirable collection of essays gathered by François Mauriac under the title *Du côté de chez Proust* is full of it. No end of sayings are there which go straight to the heart of the question. Proust, he says, died of this mighty travail—"He died, it may be, without God, whose love would have turned him, as it turned Pascal, away from any human goal." And further on the fearful words, "Does such creative work involve to some degree a renunciation of God? The question arises even for *Le Partage de Midi*, even for the *Divina Commedia*. And it is not answered by saying that this is true of everything which, not being God, turns us away from God. Our problem goes far beyond that of ordinary distractions: to write *Parsifal* is more dangerous than to play cards or work at mathematics. The creation by an artist of a work of art involves an absorption of the total being, an inattention to everything else. Like all miracles the perfect union of Grace and Art is a possibility, but so rare that it is unwise to pin our hopes upon its happening. It is not grace that is lacking, or the art that is lacking, but that in their essence the two harmonize ill. Mauriac's description of the man of letters applies to any saint—"He has made an idol of his work and the idol has devoured him." The only other possible issue is for grace to devour the idol, but an artist needs immense heroism to consent to this. It is not solely a matter of courage. He who began by sacrificing everything to art will want to concentrate upon God to the ignoring of art, as formerly upon art to the ignoring of God. He is afraid, something tells him, that in actual fact if he becomes a saint, he will cease to be an artist. "My God," Jacques Rivière wrote, "take away from me the temptation of sanctity. It is not my job." His job was certainly to be a writer. God is a temptation against art as art is a temptation against God.

And this is why many artists, not all of them second-rate, finding that art's term lay in its very endlessness, have resolutely passed beyond it. Their lives end in silence. From that hour says the biographer, he was finished. It may be so, but the man may begin where the artist ends. Valéry never forgave Pascal for that final renunciation, which he viewed as a betrayal, but surely the value of Pascal's work lies in that very element which was already beckoning him towards that renunciation. The noblest art partakes of something beyond itself. But the perfection of Valéry's work, with its total and grievous lack of spiritual grandeur, is a perfection completely contained in the sphere of art, with no summons from outside to pass beyond. Bounarotti in his old age sometimes smashed his statues: art satisfied him no longer, he was athirst for the infinite. "Neither painting nor sculpture," he said, "can thrill the soul that has turned towards that divine love who opened his arms to us upon the Cross."

Rodin, who quotes this saying of Michelangelo, adds that the words are those of the *Imitation of Christ*: "It is the highest wisdom to reach out towards the kingdom of heaven by contempt of the world. How vain to cling to what passes away so quickly and not to hasten towards joy unending."

Michelangelo, the *Imitation*, Rodin—it is a notable meeting. But do they in fact meet? Rodin at least was not shocked by Michelangelo for destroying a masterpiece because it did not express what can be expressed only by prayer. Perhaps Rodin glimpsed in the depths of his own heart a hidden longing for a God whose name was unknown to him but whom he was dimly seeking in so many works of art, wherein form is so manifestly subordinated to the demands of spirit. But this path offers no way out. As long as art is for the artist the final end, or the one path thereto, he will never reach sanctity.

The beauty of art is divine, but no artist however great is allowed to serve the divine under that one form only—a beauty the quality of which is enhanced by his own toil. And on his side the total gift of self to his work, the asceticism and self-abnegation evidenced by his triumph, make it much harder for him than for others not to feel that he has reached the end towards which his being is aiming. His life is so good a copy of sanctity that he is apt to deceive himself about its real nature. The greater the man, the more pardonable the mistake, but it still remains a mistake to fancy you can become a saint merely by dint of being an artist. Fra Angelico would have been just as happy had he painted shoes and chairs instead of painting God, the angels, and the saints. He prayed with his hands. To serve God through art is all the more difficult because the urge towards perfection always alive in the heart of the genuine artist is an irresistible temptation to serve art as if it were a god.

When it comes to a question of the final end, a choice must he made. For us, who are neither saints nor artists, the choice is easy. We are not involved as they are in a drama where the actors must hesitate between two absolutes: our very littleness enables us to see so clearly which of the two towering peaks is the higher. The artist hesitates, goes back on his choice and often ends by condemning the decision on which he acted. There can be no real proof of its validity either for him or for us. Yet perhaps his only mistake is to think himself mistaken. But who would dare to affirm it? Remember Lèon Bloy's letter to a friend in 1915: "I might have become a saint and a miracle-worker. I became a man of letters. I did not do what God wanted of me, that is certain."

No, it is by no means certain. If God had willed it, Lèon Bloy would have been a saint, but the surest way of making his sanctity certain would obviously have been not to dower him with the vast prophetic imagination and the literary gifts in the first place. Once he had them it was scarcely possible not to use them. So it is not certain—but it is possible. It may be that, of all the gifts God gives to man, the most bitter to offer in sacrifice is creative genius. Does God even desire the sacrifice of a gift so beautiful and so divine? Divine love appears divided against itself in a heart torn with this agonizing question.

Whatever way the drama be interpreted, art is not debased if we see around the summit of its greatest works the dim halo of possible sanctity. Hence comes that light with which some masterpieces are flooded and which, while still leaving them in the realm of art, bestows on them a share in the only order that is more excellent. Art, like holiness, brings the gift of tears. Why do they spring forth as though grace had wholly absorbed nature while we listen to a phrase of Mozart or a poem of Racine? A spirituality, absolute in its own order, is here flowing into the ocean that contains all spirituality. Poetry even at its purest is not prayer; but it rises from the same depths as the need to pray.

The themes meet here whose intersection makes up the very substance of the stories of these muses: for they end abruptly with the dispersing of that fruitful illusion which gave them life. We were asking, apropos of Wagner, what proportion these various stories had of sincerity and of artifice, of love of the beloved and of love of art. But it is all one and the same; directly these great poetic passions are seen as totally different from ordinary love of the senses, we know that we are in presence of a totally different love, of which no finite being can be, or even wish to be, the final end.

To love, says the Socrates of Brice Parain, "is by definition to be seeking in and through another person, expecting from another, a revelation—which he does not possess, yet which will come through him and for which he is necessary." Is it not enough splendor for anyone to be chosen as a necessary channel for a promised revelation? In this meaning the beloved is indeed "the only woman" for her poet, because in her alone the Muse has taken flesh. But it is the promise he loves in the woman, not the revelation, for this is what she never is. Unless, therefore, death transforms the woman into pure essence of inspiration, the Muse disappears when she has kept her promise—when the work of art is born. And even then the truly inspired poet is not satisfied. His most perfect art does not wholly fulfill a promise which can be fulfilled by nothing material, be it the woman or the work. It is then that he sees clearly the real object of his quest: art sought through his Muse, and God through his art.

CLUNY MEDIA

Designed by Fiona Cecile Clarke, the Cluny Media *logo*
depicts a monk at work in the scriptorium,
with a cat sitting at his feet.

The monk represents our mission to emulate
the invaluable contributions of the monks
of Cluny in preserving the libraries of the West,
our strivings to know and love the truth.

The cat at the monk's feet is Pangur Bán, from the
eponymous Irish poem of the 9th century.
The anonymous poet compares his scholarly
pursuit of truth with the cat's happy hunting of mice.
The depiction of Pangur Bán is an homage to the work
of the monks of Irish monasteries and a sign
of the joy we at Cluny take in our trade.

"Messe ocus Pangur Bán,
cechtar nathar fria saindan:
bíth a menmasam fri seilgg,
mu memna céin im saincheirdd."